I0485768

CYBERSECURITY: THE EVOLVING NATURE OF CYBER THREATS FACING THE PRIVATE SECTOR

HEARING

BEFORE THE

SUBCOMMITTEE ON INFORMATION TECHNOLOGY

OF THE

COMMITTEE ON OVERSIGHT AND GOVERNMENT REFORM HOUSE OF REPRESENTATIVES

ONE HUNDRED FOURTEENTH CONGRESS

FIRST SESSION

MARCH 18, 2015

Serial No. 114–11

Printed for the use of the Committee on Oversight and Government Reform

Available via the World Wide Web: http://www.fdsys.gov
http://www.house.gov/reform

U.S. GOVERNMENT PUBLISHING OFFICE

94–349 PDF   WASHINGTON : 2015

For sale by the Superintendent of Documents, U.S. Government Publishing Office
Internet: bookstore.gpo.gov   Phone: toll free (866) 512–1800; DC area (202) 512–1800
Fax: (202) 512–2104   Mail: Stop IDCC, Washington, DC 20402–0001

(III)

CONTENTS

CYBERSECURITY: THE EVOLVING NATURE OF CYBER THREATS FACING THE PRIVATE SECTOR

Wednesday, March 18, 2015,

HOUSE OF REPRESENTATIVES,
SUBCOMMITTEE ON INFORMATION TECHNOLOGY,
COMMITTEE ON OVERSIGHT AND GOVERNMENT REFORM,
Washington, DC.

The subcommittee met, pursuant to notice, at 1:01 p.m. in room 2154, Rayburn House Office Building, the Honorable Will Hurd (chairman of the subcommittee), presiding.

Present: Representatives Hurd, Carter, Kelly, Duckworth and Cummings.

MR. HURD. The Subcommittee on Information Technology will come to order.

Without objection, the Chair is authorized to declare a recess at any time.

Good afternoon and welcome, everyone. I appreciate you all being here.

It is great to finally be here. This hearing has been rescheduled a number of times. Hopefully, this is the first of many hearings for this Subcommittee on Information Technology within Oversight and Government Reform.

As we all know, the Oversight Committee exists because of two fundamental principles. First, Americans have a right to know that the money Washington takes from them is well spent. Second, Americans deserve an efficient and effective government that works for them.

I thank all the members for being here this afternoon. I would especially like to thank the Ranking Member, Ms Kelly, for her efforts on behalf of the committee thus far. It has been great working with you already and I am looking forward to the next year and a half.

As the Chairman of the IT Subcommittee, we are looking to do four things over this Congress. One of those issues we will look at is IT procurement and acquisition.

When I was running for Congress, I never thought I would be talking about IT procurement as much as I do but it is an important area where we can reduce the size and scope of the Federal Government.

The second area we will look at is emerging technologies. Our technology landscape is shifting and with emerging technologies such as drones, 3-D printing, these are all things that the government has not dealt in before.

We have to make sure that we are not stifling any growth in these areas, but are protecting consumers as well.

The third area we will look at is privacy. I know we will have a conversation today about this issue. When information is becoming increasingly accessible to folks and the masses, we need to make sure that we are protecting our information. We can protect our digital infrastructure and our civil liberties at the same time.

I am looking forward to delving into this topic over these next few months.

The fourth area we will talk about today is cybersecurity and information sharing. I think the Federal Government should be doing everything it can to share information with the private sector so that the private sector can protect itself.

I spent 9 years as an undercover officer in the CIA. My background is in computer science. I may be able to bang out some Fortran 77 code right now but it has been great having that experience and background and using it to help us as we chart our course forward.

I also helped build a cybersecurity company. One of the things we always tell our clients is that in this day and age, you have to begin with the presumption of breach. If you give me enough time and money, I am going to get in. What do you do to detect someone on your network? How can you contain them and then kick them out?

I think the conversation today is pretty timely with the recent attacks on Sony, Anthem, J.P. Morgan Chase and other big names. Just yesterday, we found out about 11 million customers who may have had their health records compromised in an attack on Blue Cross that occurred last May.

With each passing day and week, there is a new hack, a new breach or a theft being committed over the Internet. Because of this, we must encourage the sharing of cyber threat information to help deal with those breaches when they occur.

Having been on both the private side and the public side of this issue, I know that both sides are not communicating as well as they could be. I hope this committee can shed light on the growing problem and work with the authorizing committees and the appropriators on bringing forth beneficial cyber legislation.

The goal of today's hearing is to paint a picture of common threats, understand how the Federal Government can better engage with the private sector and get some suggestions and prescriptive measures that the Federal Government should take.

I want to thank everyone again for being here and participating today in this important hearing.

Mr. HURD. With that, I would like to now recognize my friend, the ranking member of the subcommittee, Ms. Kelly of Illinois, for 5 minutes for an opening Statement.

Ms. KELLY. Thank you, Mr. Chairman. I too look forward to working with you over the next year and a half.

Thank you, Mr. Chairman, for holding this hearing on cybersecurity threats faced by the private sector. As you just said, the announcement of the attack against Blue Cross reminds us that no company is immune from cyber attacks and data breaches.

Sophisticated companies such as Sony, Home Depot, Target, Anthem and USIS were all targeted and breached by cyber attackers. The most recent attack against Anthem, one of the Nation's leading health insurers, resulted in an attack on up to 80 million personal records of customers and employees.

That attack is particularly disturbing because, as I pointed out in an article I wrote in Roll Call last month, medical identity theft represents a new norm in cyber crime. The real victims of cyber crime are the employees and customers whose sensitive personal information is stolen and used by cyber thieves in other crimes.

Cyber theft of social security numbers, birth dates and sensitive medical information puts individuals at heightened risk of crimes such as financial fraud and tax refund fraud.

Corporations collect and utilize a lot of personal information about their customers and employees. It is imperative that those businesses employ more effective means to safeguard it.

I look forward to hearing from today's witnesses about best practices they are recommending to help their members protect against cyber attacks and mitigate any damage from data breaches.

Today's hearing is also a recognition of the fact that the Federal Government and private sector must work more effectively together to thwart cyber crime.

I also look forward to hearing from today's witnesses about what government can do to help protect businesses and consumers from future cyber attacks and data breaches.

It is worth noting that the President recently issued a series of new initiatives to improve cyber security information sharing between the government and private sector to better assist in thwarting cyber attacks. I applaud him for that but Congress needs to do more.

Thank you again, Mr. Chairman. I yield the balance of my time.

Mr. HURD. The gentlewoman yields the balance of her time.

I will hold the record open for five legislative days for any members who would like to submit written Statements.

Now we get to recognize our panel of witnesses. This is a great panel. This is actually one of those issues where I think the House, the Senate and the White House can work together. We are looking forward to that opportunity.

I am pleased to welcome our witnesses: Mr. Richard Bejtlich, Chief Security Strategist at FireEye; Mr. David French, Senior Vice President, Government Relations, National Retail Federation; Mr. Daniel Nutkis, CEO and founder of the Health Information Trust Alliance; Mr. Doug Johnson, Senior Vice President and Chief Advisor, Payments and Cybersecurity Policy, of the American Bankers Association; and Mr. Edmund Mierzwinski, Consumer Program Director and Senior Fellow, U.S. Public Interest Research Group. I want to welcome everyone here today.

Pursuant to committee rules, all witnesses will be sworn before they testify. Please rise and raise your right hand.

Do you solemnly swear or affirm that the testimony you are about to give will be the truth, the whole truth, and nothing but the truth?

[Witnesses respond in the affirmative.]

Mr. HURD. In order to allow time for discussion, please limit your testimony to 5 minutes. Your entire written Statement will be made a part of the record.

With that, Mr. Bejtlich, we will start off with you.

WITNESS STATEMENTS

STATEMENT OF RICHARD BEJTLICH

Mr. BEJTLICH. Chairman Hurd, Ranking Member Kelly, members of the committee, thank you for the opportunity to testify.

I am Richard Bejtlich, Chief Security Strategist at FireEye. Today I will discuss digital threats, how to think about risk and some strategies to address these challenges.

Who is the threat? In our work, we have discovered and countered nation-State actors from China, Russia, Iran, North Korea, Syria, and other countries.

The Chinese and Russians tend to hack for commercial and geopolitical gain. The Iranians and North Koreans extend these activities to include disruption via denial of service and sabotage using destructive malware.

Activity from Syria relates to the regional civil war and sometimes affects Western news outlets and other victims. Eastern Europe continues to be a source of criminal operations, and we worry that the conflict between Ukraine and Russia will extend into the digital realm.

Threat attribution, or identifying responsibility for a breach, depends on the political stakes surrounding an incident.

For high-profile intrusions, such as those in the news over the last few months, attribution has been a priority. National technical means, law enforcement, and counter-intelligence can pierce anonymity. Some elements of the private sector have the right experience and evidence to assist with this process.

I would like to emphasize that attribution is possible, but it is a function of what is at stake.

Who is being breached? In March 2014, the Washington Post reported that in 2013, Federal agents, often the FBI, notified more than 3,000 U.S. companies that their computer systems had been hacked. This count represents clearly identified breach victims. Many were likely compromised more than once.

In the 18 or so years I have been doing this work, this to me is the single best statistic we have because these were not attacks, these were not near misses, these were actual, serious breaches that merited notification by law enforcement.

How do victims learn of a breach? Unfortunately, in 70 percent of cases, someone else, likely the FBI, tells a victim about a serious compromise. Only 30 percent of the time do victims identify intrusions on their own.

The median amount of time from when an intruder's initial compromise, to the time when a victim learns of a breach, according to our research, is currently 205 days. This number is better last year's research where the number was 229 days. Unfortunately, it means that, for nearly 7 months after gaining initial entry, intruders are free to roam within victim networks.

What are you supposed to do about this? I like to first think of defining the risk. In this hearing, we are thinking about the risk of intrusion to private companies in the United States, but there are many other risks we could talk about. That is the focus of this hearing.

Step two is to try to figure out some ways to measure progress. When I work with companies, I try to encourage them to think in terms of a couple metrics.

The first one is how many intrusions are occurring because there are many intrusions occurring in companies but not all of them rise to the level of somebody stealing your data or somebody destroying your data.

Second, they need to track the amount of time that elapses from when the intrusion first occurs and when they do something about it. We want to drive down both of those numbers.

Some things happen outside companies which impact the threat and the cost to the intrusion. Law enforcement and counter intelligence are the primary means by which you can mitigate the threat.

I did an editorial for Brookings recently called Target Malware Kingpins where I asked what makes more sense, expecting 2 billion Internet users to adequately secure their personal information or reducing the threat posed by the approximately 100 malware kingpins in the world?

Reducing the cost side of the equation takes a little more creativity. One step—I noticed it in the testimony of some of my fellow panelists—is tokenization of payment card data such that you are not dealing in credit cards when you are trying to authorize transactions.

A second step would be to drastically reduce or preferably eliminate the value of a Social Security number. With a Social Security number, as noted in the testimony in more detail by my colleagues, you can get credit reports and just an opening to much more damage.

In brief, at least from the perspective of a private company, we can win when we stop intruders from achieving their objectives. It is ideal to prevent an adversary from getting into your network but that goal is increasingly difficult.

Instead, we need to focus on quickly detecting the intrusion, containing the adversary and stopping him before he destroys, steals or whatever his mission is, as Chairman Hurd mentioned.

Finally, we must appreciate that the time to find and remove intruders is now. If you were to hire me to be your CSO, the first step I would take would be to hunt for intruders already in your network.

I look forward to your questions.

[Prepared Statement of Mr. Bejtlich follows:]

Statement for the Record

Richard Bejtlich

Chief Security Strategist

FireEye, Inc.

Before the

U.S. House of Representatives Committee on Oversight and

Government Reform Subcommittee on Information Technology

Cybersecurity:

The Evolving Nature of Cyber Threats Facing the Private Sector

March 18, 2015

Chairman Hurd, members of the Committee, thank you for the opportunity to testify. I am Richard Bejtlich, Chief Security Strategist at FireEye. I am also a nonresident senior fellow at the Brookings Institution, and I am pursuing a PhD in war studies from King's College London. I began my security career as a military intelligence officer in 1997 at the Air Force Information Warfare Center.

My employer, FireEye, provides software to stop digital intruders, with 3,100 customers in 67 countries, including 200 of the Fortune 500. Our Mandiant consulting service, known for its 2013 report on Chinese PLA Unit 61398, helps companies identify and recover from intrusions.

Today I will discuss digital threats, how to think about risk, and some strategies to address these challenges.

Who is the threat?

We have discovered and countered nation-state actors from China, Russia, Iran, North Korea, Syria, and other countries. The Chinese and Russians tend to hack for commercial and geopolitical gain. The Iranians and North Koreans extend these activities to include disruption via denial of service and sabotage using destructive malware. Activity from Syria relates to the regional civil war and sometimes affects Western news outlets and other victims. Eastern Europe continues to be a source of criminal operations, and we worry that the conflict between Ukraine and Russia will extend into the digital realm.

Threat attribution, or identifying responsibility for a breach, depends on the political stakes surrounding an incident.[1] For high-profile intrusions, such as those in the news over the last few months, attribution has been a priority. National technical means, law enforcement, and counter-intelligence can pierce anonymity. Some elements of the private sector have the right experience and evidence to assist with this process. Attribution is possible, but it is a function of what is at stake.

Who is being breached?

---

[1] Thomas Rid and Ben Buchanan, "Attributing Cyber Attacks," The Journal of Strategic Studies, 2014; http://bit.ly/attributing-cyber-attacks

In March 2014, the Washington Post reported that in 2013, federal agents, often the FBI, notified more than 3,000 U.S. companies that their computer systems had been hacked.[2] This count represents clearly identified breach victims. Many were likely compromised more than once.

Serious intruders target more than government, defense, and financial victims. No sector is immune. FireEye recently published two reports, showing that 96% of organizations we could observe had suffered compromise during two six-month periods.[3] The best performing sector was aerospace and defense, with "only" 76% of sampled organizations suffering a breach. All of the retail, automotive, transportation, healthcare, pharmaceutical, construction, and engineering clients we passively monitored over a six-month period were breached at least once.

In 2014, the top sectors assisted by our Mandiant consultants included business and professional services, finance, media and entertainment, and construction and engineering. Many of these attacks are driven by strategic national imperatives. For instance, we anticipate that certain foreign governments will continue to steal clean energy and biotechnology solutions, so long as their citizens suffer polluted cities and rising cancer rates. Some actors specifically target the healthcare sector. Criminal groups appear to steal data for financial gain, while nation-state hackers may steal data to improve the healthcare systems of their own countries, or to support national commercial champions.

How are victims breached?

Intruders use spear phishing, attacks against Internet-connected devices, and other methods to compromise victims. Last year we observed a rise in the proportion of phishing emails that impersonated IT staff, from 44% in 2013 to 78% in 2014.[4] The threat is going mobile as well. We recently completed a study of vulnerable mobile applications that can hijack entire devices, without the user's knowledge. We have seen malicious applications, pretending to offer banking services, harvest credentials and steal two-factor authentication codes and virtual private network passwords.

---

[2] Ellen Nakashima, "U.S. notified 3,000 companies in 2013 about cyberattacks," Washington Post, March 24, 2014; http://www.washingtonpost.com/world/national-security/2014/03/24/74aff686-aed9-11e3-96dc-d6ea14c099f9_story.html

[3] https://www.fireeye.com/blog/executive-perspective/2015/01/the_maginot_linedee.html

[4] https://www.fireeye.com/blog/threat-research/2015/02/get_a_view_from_the.html

How do victims learn of a breach?

In 70% of cases, someone else, likely the FBI, tells a victim about a serious compromise. Only 30% of the time do victims identify intrusions on their own. The median amount of time from an intruder's initial compromise, to the time when a victim learns of a breach, is currently 205 days, as reported in our 2015 M-Trends report. This number is better than our 229 day count for 2013, and the 243 day count for 2012.[5] Unfortunately, it means that, for nearly 7 months after gaining initial entry, intruders are free to roam within victim networks.

What is the answer?

Before talking about solutions to digital risk, we need to define it. Always ask "Risk of what?" Are we talking about the risk of a teenager committing suicide due to "cyber bu lying," or the risk of a retiree's 401k being emptied due to electronic theft, or the risk of a week-long power outage due to state-sponsored attack?

Step one is to define the risk, and step two is to measure progress by combining ways and means to achieve defined ends. This is exactly the role of strategic thinking, meaning the application of strategies, campaigns, tactics and tools to achieve organizational goals.

For example, a company may worry about the risk of losing intellectual property to foreign hackers. The board and management team works with the chief security officer (CSO) to define a company goal of minimizing loss due to digital intrusions. To accomplish the goal, they agree on a strategy of rapid incident detection and response. To achieve the strategy, the CSO develops a campaign to hunt for intruders in the company using network security monitoring (NSM) operations. To prosecute the campaign, the security team implements tactics to collect, analyze, escalate, and resolve intrusions based on NSM principles. Finally, the security team uses tools, or security software, to bring their tactics to life.[6]

---

[5] https://www.mandiant.com/resources/mandiant-reports/
[6] http://taosecurity.blogspot.com/search/label/strategy

To measure success, the security team should track the number of intrusions that occur per year, and the amount of time that elapses from the initial entry point to the time of discovery, and from the time of discovery to the removal of the threat. This strategic approach is the reason Mandiant calculates these metrics when helping breach victims.

Security professionals define Risk as the product of Threat, Vulnerability, and Cost, which is the impact of a security incident. We use a pseudo-equation where R = T x V x C. We're not trying to calculate a number. We're trying to show how Threat, Vulnerability, and Cost influence Risk. If any factor increases, Risk increases, and if any factor decreases, Risk decreases. We appear to live in an environment where Threat, Vulnerability, and Cost continue to rise, driving up Risk, but note that reducing any component -- Threat, Vulnerability, or Cost -- helps lower Risk.

Too often the more engineering-focused members of the security community fixate on Vulnerability. We hear of "game-changing technologies" promising to remove flaws, reduce attack surfaces, and so on. While I accept the need for more secure software, we must not neglect the role of reducing the Threat and the Cost they impose.

Law enforcement and counter-intelligence operations are the primary means by which we can mitigate the Threat. In an editorial for the Brookings Institution titled "Target Malware Kingpins," I asked "what makes more sense: expecting the two billion Internet users worldwide to adequately secure their personal information, or reducing the threat posed by the roughly 100 top-tier malware authors?"[7] Along those lines, I applaud the FBI's recent announcement of a $3 million bounty for information leading to the arrest of a Russian hacking suspect who stole more than $100 million since 2011.[8]

Reducing the Cost of security incidents takes somewhat more creative approaches. One step in progress is the "tokenization" of the payment card system, whereby strings of numbers, or "tokens," replace traditional credit card numbers. A second step would be eliminating the value of Social Security numbers to identify thieves. I recommend reading the Electronic Privacy Information Center's suggestions on "effective SSN legislation" for policy changes.[9]

---

[7] Richard Bejtlich, "Target Malware Kingpins," The Brookings Institution; http://www.brookings.edu/research/opinions/2015/02/02-cybersecurity-target-malware-kingpins-bejtlich
[8] http://www.fbi.gov/wanted/cyber/evgeniy-mikhailovich-bogachev
[9] https://epic.org/privacy/ssn/

In brief, defenders win when they stop intruders from achieving their objectives. It's ideal to stop the adversary from entering the network, but that goal is increasingly difficult. If traditional defenses fail, you must quickly detect the intrusion, and respond to contain the adversary, before he steals, changes, or destroys the data or system under attack.

Finally, we must appreciate that the time to find and remove intruders is now. There is no point in planning for theoretical, future breaches until you know your own, current, security posture. If a company hired me to be their CSO, the first step I would take would be to hunt for intruders already in the network.

I look forward to your questions.

Richard Bejtlich

Chief Security Strategist at FireEye, Inc.

taosecurity@gmail.com

Summary

Richard Bejtlich is Chief Security Strategist at FireEye, and was Mandiant's Chief Security Officer when FireEye acquired Mandiant in 2013. He is a nonresident senior fellow at the Brookings Institution, a board member at the Open Information Security Foundation, and an advisor to Threat Stack, Sqrrl, and Critical Stack. He is also a Master/Doctor of Philosophy in War Studies Researcher at King's College London. He was previously Director of Incident Response for General Electric, where he built and led the 40-member GE Computer Incident Response Team (GE-CIRT). Richard began his digital security career as a military intelligence officer in 1997 at the Air Force Computer Emergency Response Team (AFCERT), Air Force Information Warfare Center (AFIWC), and Air Intelligence Agency (AIA). Richard is a graduate of Harvard University and the United States Air Force Academy. His fourth book is "The Practice of Network Security Monitoring" (nostarch.com/nsm). He also writes for his blog (taosecurity.blogspot.com) and Twitter (@taosecurity).

Experience

Master/Doctor Of Philosophy In War Studies Researcher at King's College London
August 2014 - Present (7 months)

Researching application of strategic thought, especially operational art, to counter-intrusion campaigns. The research will identify elements of a successful computer network defense campaign, inspired by both classical and modern thinkers.

Advisor at Critical Stack
August 2014 - Present (7 months)

Advises Critical Stack on business strategy, product opportunities, communications, and other commercial organizational issues.

Advisor at Sqrrl
June 2014 - Present (9 months)

Advises Sqrrl on business strategy, product opportunities, communications, and other commercial organizational issues.

Chief Security Strategist at FireEye, Inc.
January 2014 - Present (1 year 2 months)

Empowers policy makers, international leaders, global customers, and concerned citizens to understand and mitigate digital risk through strategic security programs.

Nonresident Senior Fellow at The Brookings Institution
January 2014 - Present (1 year 2 months)

Researches integrating strategic thought into private sector cyber defense. Investigates the extent to which
detection and response scales beyond the enterprise.

Advisor at Threat Stack, Inc
October 2013 - Present (1 year 5 months)

Advises Threat Stack on business strategy, product opportunities, communications, and other commercial
organizational issues.

Board Member at The Open Information Security Foundation
March 2011 - Present (4 years)

Advises OISF on business strategy, product development, communications, and other non-profit
organizational issues. Advocates use of OISF open source software like Suricata to complement computer
security programs worldwide.

Chief Security Officer at Mandiant
April 2011 - January 2014 (2 years 10 months)

Managed Mandiant's digital risks, advocated defenses against advanced threats, and helped customers detect
and respond to intrusions using the company's methods, products, and services. Transitioned to FireEye after
acquisition of Mandiant in December 2013.

Director, Incident Response at General Electric
July 2007 - April 2011 (3 years 0 months)

Built and led GE Computer Incident Response Team (GE-CIRT, ge.com/cirt) from 0 to 40 analysts,
defending 300,000 employees and 500,000 nodes in over 100 countries.

President & CEO at TaoSecurity LLC
June 2005 - June 2007 (2 years 1 month)

Provided independent digital security consulting and services for military, government, and commercial
clients worldwide.

1 recommendation available upon request

Technical Director at ManTech International Corp.
February 2004 - June 2005 (1 year 5 months)

Performed computer forensics and intrusion analysis for government clients, and network security monitoring
for corporate customers.

Principal Consultant at Foundstone
April 2002 - January 2004 (1 year 10 months)

Led incident response engagements for Fortune 100, tier one ISPs, and other organized crime and corporate
espionage victims.

1 recommendation available upon request

Senior Security Engineer at Ball Aerospace & Technologies Corp.

February 2001 - April 2002 (1 year 3 months)

Designed, hired, trained, and led a twelve-person, 24x7 team to detect intrusions on commercial networks.

Chief, Real Time Intrusion Detection at AFCERT

September 1998 - February 2001 (2 years 6 months)

Led Air Force CERT's security monitoring mission, supervising 60 civilian and military staff; conducted hands-on technical analysis.

2 recommendations available upon request

Intelligence Officer at Air Intelligence Agency

February 1997 - September 1998 (1 year 8 months)

Created and coordinated information warfare plans and policies, and executed operations during Bosnia conflict.

Skills & Expertise

Computer Forensics
Intrusion Detection
Corporate Security
Security Operations
Security Services
Managed Security Services
Cyber Security
Security Management
Information Security Management
Internet Security
CISSP
Computer Security
Network Security
Security Research
Network Forensics
Security
IDS

Patents

Network intrusion detection visualization

United States Patent Application 20110067106

Inventors: Richard Bejtlich, Scott Evans, Et al

Network attack visualization and response through intelligent icons

United States Patent Application 20110066409

Inventors: Richard Bejtlich, Scott Evans, Et al

Publications

The Practice of Network Security Monitoring
No Starch   July 22, 2013
Authors: Richard Bejtlich

In The Practice of Network Security Monitoring, Mandiant CSO Richard Bejtlich shows you how to use NSM to add a robust layer of protection around your networks — no prior experience required. To help you avoid costly and inflexible solutions, he teaches you how to deploy, build, and run an NSM operation using open source software and vendor-neutral tools.

Extrusion Detection
Addison-Wesley   November 8, 2005
Authors: Richard Bejtlich

Real Digital Forensics
Addison-Wesley   September 23, 2004
Authors: Richard Bejtlich, Keith Jones, Curtis Rose

The Tao of Network Security Monitoring
Addison-Wesley   July 12, 2004
Authors: Richard Bejtlich

Education

Air Force Intelligence Officers Training Course
14N1, Military intelligence, 1996 - 1997

Harvard University, John F. Kennedy School of Government
Master of Public Policy (MPP), National Security, 1994 - 1996

United States Air Force Academy
Bachelor of Science (BS), History, Political Science, 1990 - 1994
Grade: 3rd of 1024
Activities and Societies: French and German minors

Committee on Oversight and Government Reform
Witness Disclosure Requirement – "Truth in Testimony"
Required by House Rule XI, Clause 2(g)(5)

Name: **Richard Bejtlich**

1. Please list any federal grants or contracts (including subgrants or subcontracts) you have received since October 1, 2012. Include the source and amount of each grant or contract.

FireEye has multiple contracts with numerous US Federal government agencies and foreign governments for cybersecurity products and services which are relevant to the subject matter of this hearing. Pursuant to these agreements, FireEye is subject to non-disclosure provisions.

2. Please list any entity you are testifying on behalf of and briefly describe your relationship with these entities.

I represent my employer, FireEye, Inc.

3. Please list any federal grants or contracts (including subgrants or subcontracts) received since October 1, 2012, by the entity(ies) you listed above. Include the source and amount of each grant or contract.

FireEye has multiple contracts with numerous US Federal government agencies and foreign governments for cybersecurity products and services which are relevant to the subject matter of this hearing. Pursuant to these agreements, FireEye is subject to non-disclosure provisions.

I certify that the above information is true and correct.

Signature:

Date: 2 March 2015

Mr. HURD. Thank you, Mr. Bejtlich.

The Chair now recognizes Mr. French.

STATEMENT OF DAVID FRENCH

Mr. FRENCH. Thank you for the opportunity to provide you with our views on cyber security threats facing the private sector as well as achievable solutions to better protect sensitive information.

Retailers are just one of the targets in an evolving and escalating war on our digital economy. Merchants collectively spend billions of dollars safeguarding sensitive customer information.

At the outset, let me State that data intrusion is a crime of a particularly international character. In virtually every reported incident, it seems as if the criminals are operating from abroad beyond the reach of U.S. law enforcement.

In all of the congressional scrutiny over data security, there has been a conspicuous lack of attention paid to strengthening our national ability to interdict and prosecute these criminals. We do not have specific recommendations in this area but it is an observation that this committee is uniquely well situated to conduct such an inquiry.

Beyond better law enforcement tools, my remarks center on three themes: better payment card security; effective breach notification and sharing of cyber threat information.

In our view, security alone is not the answer. The issue must be considered much more holistically. We must work together to prevent cyber attacks and help reduce fraud or other economic harm that may result when breaches occur.

Ultimately, we must make data less valuable. If breaches become less profitable to criminals, then criminals will dedicate fewer resources to committing them and our common data security goals will become much more achievable.

Cyber attacks are a fact of life in the United States. Virtually every network is at risk. In its 2014 data breach investigation report, Verizon determined that there were more than 63,000 data security incidents reported by industry, educational institutions and government entities in 2013. Of those, more than 1,300 had confirmed data losses. The financial industry suffered 34 percent of these and the retail industry had less than 11 percent.

I do not cite these figures to criticize our colleagues in the banking industry but merely to illustrate the fact that the incidents of data breaches are proportionate to the relative value of information that can be stolen.

It should not be surprising that three times more data breaches occur at financial institutions than at retailers. Criminals seek high value information and data thieves know that banks are most sensitive to financial and personal information, including not just card numbers but bank account numbers, Social Security numbers and other identified data that can be used to steal identities beyond completing some fraudulent transaction.

When it comes to payment card data, there is one single fact that banks and the card networks must acknowledge. All of the decisions about card design and security are theirs alone. Retailers did not forgo chip technology in the U.S. for almost two decades and we did not conceive of the complex, costly and largely ineffective payment card industry data security standards. We have to live with the downstream costs of these decisions every day.

Without fraud-prone payment card information and retailer systems, criminals would find the rest of the information retailers typically hold and that is benign data such as phone book information, shoe size or color preferences to be all that interesting or more importantly, lucrative on the black market.

That is why payment card security is essential and the adoption of a microchip in payment cards is a long overdue step in the right direction.

For retailers, however, the debate over card security comes down to a basic question about why the card networks and banks continue to rely on signature-based authentication methods rather than the proven security of a four digit personal identification number of pin.

Around the globe, most industrialized nations have adopted pin-based solutions. We know that pins provide an extra layer of security against downstream fraud, even if the card numbers are stolen in a breach.

In pin-based transactions, for example, the stored 16 digits from the card would alone be insufficient to conduct a fraudulent transaction in a store without the four digit pin which is known to the consumer and not present on the card itself. In short, the value of the pin is hard to question.

It is clear to retailers that simple business practices improvements like eliminating signature and adopting pin would be easier and more quickly implemented than any other steps. They hold the promise of being more effective in preventing the kind of financial harm that could impact consumers as companies suffer data security breaches affecting payment cards in the future.

NRF also commends the President's recent Executive Order which called for establishing cyber threat information sharing among non-critical infrastructure industries such as retail through what are called information sharing and analysis organizations, ISAOs.

The information sharing groups proposed appear similar to the Information Technology Security Council formed by NRF last year that currently shares cyber threat information among more than 170 information security professionals in retail.

More than 2,000 cyber threat alerts have been sent to our retail members since the inception of our program and we continue to expand its reach among the retail community.

Mr. Chairman, the remainder of my comments are in my written remarks. Thank you for the opportunity to testify. I look forward to your questions.

[Prepared Statement of Mr. French follows:]

TESTIMONY OF

DAVID FRENCH

SENIOR VICE PRESIDENT, GOVERNMENT RELATIONS
NATIONAL RETAIL FEDERATION

BEFORE THE HOUSE OVERSIGHT AND GOVERNMENT REFORM
SUBCOMMITTEE ON INFORMATION TECHNOLOGY

HEARING ON

"CYBERSECURITY: THE EVOLVING NATURE OF CYBER THREATS
FACING THE PRIVATE SECTOR"

MARCH 18, 2015

National Retail Federation
1101 New York Avenue, NW
Suite 1200
Washington, DC 20005
(202) 626-8126
www.nrf.com

Chairman Hurd, Ranking Member Kelly, and members of the Subcommittee, on behalf of the National Retail Federation (NRF), I want to thank you for giving us the opportunity to testify at this hearing and provide you with our views on cybersecurity threats facing the private sector and achievable solutions that Congress and the White House may work toward in order to better protect Americans' sensitive information. NRF is the world's largest retail trade association, representing discount and department stores, home goods and specialty stores, Main Street merchants, grocers, wholesalers, chain restaurants and Internet retailers from the United States and more than 45 countries. Retail is the nation's largest private sector employer, supporting one in four U.S. jobs – 42 million working Americans. Contributing $2.6 trillion to annual GDP, retail is a daily barometer for the nation's economy.

We appreciate the committee calling this hearing at a time when all different kinds of American businesses find themselves the targets in an evolving war on our digital economy – a war in which we are unwilling combatants who must defend vigorously against attacks by both criminals and nation states. Key aspects of the cyber attacks facing the breadth of American industries are, typically, the criminal fraud motive and the foreign source of the attack. Virtually all of the data breaches we have seen in the United States during the past year – from attacks on the networked systems of retailers, entertainment and technology companies that have been prominent in the news, to a reported series of attacks on our largest banks this past summer – have been perpetrated by overseas criminals who are breaking the law. All of these breached companies are victims of these foreign-actor crimes, and we should keep this in mind as we explore the topic today and in forthcoming public policy initiatives relating to this issue. The committee – in its own oversight and investigations role – also has an important responsibility to review the efforts being made by the U.S. government to improve and enhance our extra-territorial law enforcement activities against foreign criminals that attack and breach the networked systems of businesses all across the United States.

Retailers collectively spend billions of dollars safeguarding sensitive customer information and fighting fraud that results when criminals succeed in breaching their protected information systems. Data security is something that our members place at the top of their business priorities, and securing data from increasingly sophisticated attacks is an effort that retailers, as a community, strive to improve every day. This is also an issue on which the retailer and consumer interests are aligned in protecting some of the most sensitive information retailers hold – typically, the customer's payment card number. If retailers are not good custodians of payment data related to our customers, they will no longer continue to frequent our establishments and use their credit and debit cards in our stores. When we examine the threats to all businesses, we should understand that basic underlying reason that retailers are being attacked is for payment card numbers in order to perpetrate credit card fraud.

We also urge members of the Committee to review and support legislative efforts designed to help mitigate the threat of cyber attacks as well as inform consumers of breaches of sensitive information whenever and wherever they occur. These issues are ones that we recommend you examine in a holistic fashion: we need to help prevent cyber attacks, and when attacks result in data breaches, help reduce fraud or other economic harm that may result from those breaches. We should not be satisfied with simply determining what to do after a data breach occurs – that is, who to notify and how to assign liability. Instead, it is important to look at why such breaches occur, and what the perpetrators get out of them, so that we can find ways to reduce and prevent not only the breaches themselves, but the follow-on harm that is often the criminal motive behind these attacks. If breaches become less profitable to criminals, then they will dedicate fewer resources to committing them, and our data security goals will become more achievable.

With these three guiding observations in mind, our testimony below presents six proposed solutions that would help businesses defend against cyber attacks and mitigate the harm from any resulting breaches of security. These are proposals that we believe policy makers can work together to achieve in the near term, either through consumer and industry-supported legislation, or by working with the private sector on improving security practices outside of the lawmaking process. As requested by the committee, however, we begin by providing our views below on the evolving nature of the cybersecurity threat, and the latest data showing that this threat is not unique to any one industry. Following that, we discuss, our six-point proposal, some of the technological advancements retailers have promoted that could improve the security of our networks and offer additional ways to achieve greater payment security, since the payment card data itself is what drives the attacks on the retail industry. Additionally, in our proposed solutions, we suggest some of the elements of data breach notification legislation that may provide the best approach to developing a uniform, nationwide notification standard, based on the strong consensus of state laws, which applies to all businesses that handle sensitive personal information of consumers.

A. Cyber Attacks and Data Breaches in the United States

Unfortunately, cyber attacks and data breaches are a fact of life in the United States, and virtually every part of the U.S. economy and government is being attacked in some way. In its 2014 Data Breach Investigations Report, Verizon determined there were 63,347 data security incidents reported by industry, educational institutions, and governmental entities in 2013, and that 1,367 of those had confirmed data losses. Of those, the financial industry suffered 34%, public institutions (including governmental entities) had 12.8%, the retail industry had 10.8%, and hotels and restaurants combined had 10%. The chart below illustrates where breaches occur.

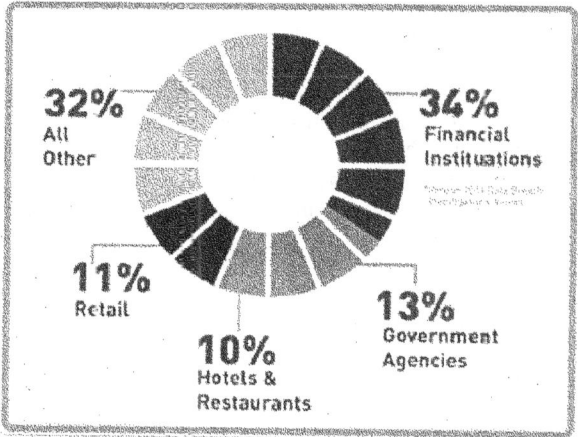

Source: 2014 Data Breach Investigations Report, Verizon[1]

---

[1] 2014 Data Breach Investigations Report by Verizon, available at: http://www.verizonenterprise.com/DBIR/2014/

As the chart above shows, the latest breach report data from Verizon reflects that three times more data breaches occur at financial institutions than at retailers. Criminals are after the most valuable information they can find, and payment card numbers – which are immediately cancelled and replaced with new number when fraud is discovered – are not as valuable as bank account information that can lead to account takeovers and/or identity theft. It should also be noted that even these percentage figures above obscure the fact that there are far more merchants that are potential targets of criminals in this area, as there are one thousand times more merchants accepting card payments in the United States than there are financial institutions issuing cards and processing those payments. It is not surprising, then, that data thieves focus far more often on banks, which hold our most sensitive financial and personal information – including not just card account numbers but bank account numbers, social security numbers and other identifying data that can be used to steal identities beyond completing some fraudulent transactions.

These figures are sobering. There are far too many attacks that result in breaches, and the breaches are often difficult to detect and are carried out in many cases by criminals with the latest technological methods at their disposal and significant resources behind them. We need to recognize that this is a continuous battle against determined fraudsters and be guided by that reality. It is also a key reason why our proposed solutions below focus on the payment card system and hardening protections against card fraud. Without fraud-prone payment card information in a retailer's system, criminals would not find the rest of the information retailers hold – benign data such as phone book information or shoe size, color preference, etc. – to be all that interesting, or more importantly, lucrative on the black market.

B. Achievable Solutions to Improving Cybersecurity

As noted above, protecting their businesses and customers from cyber attacks is of paramount importance to retailers. In today's world of networked systems, retailers also recognize that it is going to take the highest level of collaboration and coordination to make sure we do it right. That means government, industry and law enforcement alike must work together to address and defend against the attacks facing American businesses. As part of our efforts to build this collaboration necessary to succeed, NRF's President and Chief Executive Officer and Vice President for Retail Technology were on hand at The White House Summit on Cybersecurity and Consumer Protection, held at Stanford University on February 13, 2015, as President Obama announced new steps to combat an increasing number of cyber attacks that have hit targets ranging from retail stores to insurance companies to the White House itself. As the president remarked, "There's only one way to defend America from these cyber threats, and that is through government and industry working together, sharing appropriate information, as true partners."

We agree and support President Obama's call for cybersecurity threat information-sharing as a necessary element of any set of proposals to defend against cybersecurity attacks. NRF supports the passage by Congress of legislation like H.R. 624, the "Cyber Intelligence Sharing and Protection Act," cosponsored last Congress by Congressmen Rogers and Ruppersberger, which passed the House of Representatives with bipartisan support. This type of legislation would protect and create incentives for private sector entities to lawfully share cyber-threat information with other private entities and with the federal government in real-time. This would help companies better defend their own networks from cyber-attacks detected elsewhere.

NRF also commended the goals of the president's Executive Order, which called for establishing cyber threat information-sharing among non-critical infrastructure industries through Information Sharing and Analysis Organizations (ISAOs). The information-sharing groups proposed by President Obama appear similar to the Information Technology Security Council formed by NRF last year that currently shares cyber threat information among nearly 170 security professionals, such as Chief Information Security Officers (CISOs), from over 100 of the most influential retail companies. NRF has partnered with private sector and government entities to develop and disseminate cybersecurity threat indicators to our members. These partners include the Financial Services Information Sharing and Analysis Center (FS-ISAC), the United States Computer Emergency Readiness Team (US-CERT) of the Department of Homeland Security, the United States Secret Service (USSS), and the Federal Bureau of Investigation (FBI). More than 2,000 cyber threat alerts have been sent to our participating retail members since the inception of our threat information-sharing program, and we continue to expand its reach among the retail community.

In an open letter to the president that NRF published during the summit, we applauded the White House and President Obama for providing solution-based leadership around the significant threat posed by hackers and other cyber criminals. We also affirmed the retail industry's commitment to safeguarding consumer data and working with the president and Congress to achieve practical solutions to these serious problems. Our letter outlined a specific set of additional, achievable solutions that we – and every industry with a stake in the issue – must work toward in order to better protect American consumers, empower our businesses and effectively safeguard America's cyberspace against criminal hackers. Specifically, we called upon policymakers to work toward these solutions beyond the information-sharing efforts noted above:

- Support the immediate passage of FEDERAL FRAUD PROTECTION FOR DEBIT CARDS, similar to what we enjoy for credit cards. Americans should not have to pay more for fraud protection.

- Call on the payment card industry to stop relying on fraud-prone signatures and issue PIN AND CHIP CARDS for all Americans, among the least protected consumers in the world.

- Encourage all entities in the payments system — not just retailers — to ADOPT END-TO-END ENCRYPTION to protect consumers' payment information throughout the entire payments chain.

- Endorse the development of OPEN, COMPETITIVE TOKENIZATION STANDARDS to replace consumers' sensitive personal data (including payment card data) with non-sensitive "tokens" so that stored information is useless to would-be hackers.

- Continue support for a SINGLE NATIONAL DATA BREACH NOTIFICATION LAW that would establish a clear disclosure standard for all businesses to inform consumers of breaches whenever and wherever they occur.

- Support the passage of federal law enforcement legislation that would AID IN THE INVESTIGATION AND PROSECURITON OF CRIMINIALS that breach our businesses' networks and harm our consumers.

In reviewing these proposals, we ask that you consider our views in each of these six areas of achievable solutions:

1. Federal Fraud Protection for Debit Cards

From many consumers' perspective, payment cards are payment cards. As has been often noted, consumers would be surprised to learn that their legal rights, when using a debit card – i.e., their own money – are significantly less than when using other forms of payment, such as a credit card. It would be appropriate if policy makers took steps to ensure that consumers' reasonable expectations were fulfilled, and they received at least the same level of legal protection when using their debit cards as they do when paying with credit.

NRF strongly supports legislation like S. 2200, the "Consumer Debit Card Protection Act," cosponsored by Senators Warner and Kirk last Congress. S. 2200 was a bipartisan solution that would immediately provide liability protection for consumers from debit card fraud to the same extent that they are currently protected from credit card fraud. This is a long overdue correction in the law and one concrete step Congress could take immediately to protect consumers that use debit cards for payment transactions.

2. Payment Card Security – "PIN and Chip" Cards

There are many technologies available that could reduce fraud resulting from payment card breaches, and an overhaul of the fraud-prone cards that are currently used in the U.S. market is long overdue. That is because using the best network security technology and practices available does not guarantee that a business can avoid suffering a security breach which exposes sensitive data, such as payment card numbers. Therefore, raising security standards alone may not be the most efficient or effective means of preventing potential harm to consumers from card fraud. With respect to payment card numbers, for example, it is possible that no matter how much security is applied by a business storing these numbers, the numbers may be stolen from a business's database in a highly sophisticated security breach that can evade even state-of-the-art system security measures. Because of these risks, it makes sense for industry to do more than just apply increased network or database security measures.

One method to help prevent downstream fraud from stolen card numbers is to require more data or additional numbers from a consumer (such as their entry of a 4-digit personal identification number, or "PIN") to complete a payment transaction rather than simply permit the transaction to be approved on the basis of the numbers that appear on the face of a card. Requiring this type of out-of-wallet information in order to authorize and complete payment card transactions is time-tested by the banking industry, as they have required the use of PINs to access bank accounts through ATM machines for decades, a minor inconvenience that American consumers have borne for the trade-off in increased security when accessing cash. Around the globe, the most industrialized nations – the G-20 – have also adopted PIN-based solutions to replace the antiquated signature authentication methods that derive from the mid-twentieth century.

NRF believes it is time to phase out signature-authentication for all U.S.-issued payment cards – today's magnetic stripe cards as well as tomorrow's chip-based cards – and adopt a more secure authentication method for credit and debit card transactions. PINs can provide an extra layer of security against downstream fraud even if the card numbers (which the card companies already emboss on the outside of a card) are stolen in a breach. In PIN-based transactions, for example, the stored 20-digits from the card would, alone, be insufficient to conduct a fraudulent transaction in a store without the 4-digit PIN known to the consumer and not present on the card itself. These business practice improvements are easier and quicker to implement than any new federal data security law, and they hold the promise of being more effective at preventing the kind of financial harm that could impact consumers as companies suffer data security breaches affecting payment cards in the future.

In support of these concepts, on October 17, 2014, the President signed an executive order initiating the BuySecure Initiative for government payment cards.[2] The order provided, among other things, that payment cards issued to government employees would include PIN and chip technology and that government equipment to handle and process transactions would be upgraded to allow acceptance of PIN and chip. Requiring PINs for all payment card transactions, as are required for some debit and ATM transactions (and some in-bank teller transactions as well) are common-sense actions that the banking industry should adopt immediately. Retail customers – American consumers – would be better protected by the replacement of a signature – a relic of the past – with the tried-and-true PIN that all other G-20 nations, including Canada, the U.K. and our European allies have adopted as part of their card payment system to protect their citizens.

As I noted, requiring the use of a PIN is one way to reduce fraud. Doing so takes a vulnerable piece of data (the card number) and makes it so that it cannot be used on its own. This approach to payment card security should be adopted not only in the brick-and-mortar environment, in which a physical card is used, but also in the online environment in which the physical card does not have to be used. Many U.S. companies, for example, are exploring the use of a PIN for online purchases, similar to efforts underway already in Canada and Europe. Adopting PIN-like protections for online purchases may help directly with the 90 percent of U.S. fraud which occurs online.

---

[2] Executive Order – Improving the Security of Consumer Financial Transactions, The White House, October 17, 2014. Accessible at: http://www.whitehouse.gov/the-press-office/2014/10/17/executive-order-improving-security-consumer-financial-transactions

3. Network Security – "End-to-End Encryption" (or "E2E")

Encryption of payment card transaction data is another technological solution retailers employ to help defend against cyber attacks and that could help deter and prevent data breaches and the resulting fraud that can occur. Merchants are already required by Payment Card Industry (PCI) data security standards to encrypt cardholder data while being stored but, as not everyone in the entire payments chain is able to accept data in encrypted form during payment authorization, sensitive data may be left exposed (after it leaves the retailer's system in encrypted form) at a critical time in the payment process. Payment security experts have therefore called for a change to require "end-to-end" encryption, which is simply a way to describe requiring everyone in the payment-handling chain to accept, hold and transmit the payment card data in encrypted form. This would require, as the PCI standards currently require of merchants but not of others in the payment stream, that card-issuing banks, merchant banks, branded payment card networks and payment card processors all adopt the same technology to handle encrypted payment card data. In fact, knowing that card chip technology alone is not the panacea touted by branded payment card networks, many retailers are not waiting for an E2E standard, and are investing, at significant costs, in P2P Encryption[3].

According to the September 2009 issue of the Nilson Report "most recent cyberattacks have involved intercepting data in transit from the point of sale to the merchant or acquirer's host, or from that host to the payments network." The reason this often occurs is that "data must be decrypted before being forwarded to a processor or acquirer because Visa, MasterCard, American Express, and Discover networks can't accept encrypted data at this time."[4]

Keeping sensitive data encrypted throughout the payments chain would go a long way to convincing fraudsters that the data is not worth stealing in the first place – at least, not unless they were prepared to go through the arduous task of trying to de-encrypt the data which would be necessary in order to make use of it. We ask policymakers to urge our partners in the payments system, like we have, to adopt the most secure technologies to protect American consumers from card fraud. In the meantime, until all of the stakeholders in the payments system adopt technology to enable "end-to-end" encryption, using PIN-authentication of payment cards now would offer some additional protection against fraud should the decrypted payment data today be intercepted by a criminal during its transmission "in the clear."

4. Open, Competitive Tokenization Standards

Another sensible and achievable proposal to deter and protect against the harm that may result from cyber attacks is to minimize the storage and use by businesses of the full set of unredacted and unencrypted payment card numbers necessary to complete a transaction – a data protection principle known as "data minimization." For example, a decade ago, the National Retail Federation asked the branded card networks and banks to lift the requirement that retailers store full payment card numbers for all transactions.

Tokenization is a system in which sensitive payment card information (such as the account number) is replaced with another piece of data (the "token"). Sensitive payment card

---

[3] NRF Retail CIO Download, Agenda 2015: Secure and Innovate, February 2015, page 12
[4] The Nilson Report, Issue 934, Sept. 2009 at 7.

data can be replaced, for example, with a token to represent each specific transaction. Then, if a data breach occurred and the token data were stolen, it could not be used in any other transactions because it was unique to the transaction in question. This technology has been available in the payment card space since at least 2005.[5] Still, like the other proposed technological solutions above, tokenization is not a silver bullet solution, and it is important that whichever form of tokenization is adopted be one based on an open standard. This would help prevent a small number of networks from obtaining a competitive advantage, by design, over other payment platforms through the promotion of proprietary tokenization standards only.

In addition, in some configurations, mobile payments offer the promise of greater security as well. In the mobile setting, consumers would not need to have a physical payment card – and the mobile payments technology certainly would not need to replicate the security problem of physical cards that emboss account numbers on their face. It should also be easy for consumers to enter a PIN or password to use payment technology with their smart phones. Consumers are already used to accessing their phones and a variety of services on them through passwords, and increasingly, biometric finger prints. Indeed, if we are looking to leapfrog the already aging and fraud-prone current technologies, mobile-driven payments may be the answer.

Indeed, as much improved as they are, the proposed chips to be slowly rolled out on U.S. payment cards are essentially dumb computers. Their dynamism makes them significantly more advanced than magnetic stripes on most of American's payment cards today, but their sophistication pales in comparison with the sophistication of even the most basic and common smartphone. Smartphones contain computing powers that could easily enable state-of-the-art fraud protection technologies. In fact, "the new iPhones sold over the weekend of their release in September 2014 contained 25 times more computing power than the whole world had at its disposal in 1995."[6] Smart phones soon may be nearly ubiquitous, and if their payment platforms are open and competitive, they will only get better.

5. National Data Breach Notification Law

The Year of the Breach, as 2014 has been nicknamed, was replete with news stories about data security incidents that raised concerns for all American consumers and for the businesses with which they frequently interact. Criminals focused on U.S. businesses, including merchants, banks, telecom providers, cloud services providers, technology companies, and others. These criminals devoted substantial resources and expertise to breaching the most advanced data protection systems. Vigilance against these threats is necessary, but we need to focus on the underlying causes of breaches as much as we do on the effects of them.

If there is anything that the recently reported data breaches have taught us, it is that any security gaps left unaddressed will quickly be exploited by criminals. For example, the failure of the payment cards themselves to be secured by anything more sophisticated than an easily-forged signature makes the card numbers particularly attractive to criminals and the cards themselves vulnerable to fraudulent misuse. Likewise, cloud services companies that do not remove data when a customer requests its deletion, leave sensitive information available in cloud storage for

---

[5] For information on Shift4's 2005 launch of tokenization in the payment card space see
http://www.internetretailer.com/2005/10/13/shift4-launches-security-tool-that-lets-merchants-re-use-credit.
[6] "The Future of Work: There's an app for that," *The Economist* (Jan. 3, 2015).

thieves to later break in and steal, all while the customer suspects it has long been deleted. Better security at the source of the problem is needed. The protection of Americans' sensitive information is not an issue on which unreasonably limiting comprehensiveness makes any sense.

In fact, the safety of Americans' data is only as secure as the weakest link in the chain of entities that share that data for a multitude of purposes. For instance, when information moves across communications lines – for transmission or processing – or is stored in a "cloud," it would be senseless for legislation to exempt these service providers, if breached, from comparable data security and notification obligations to those that the law would place upon any other entity that suffers a breach. Likewise, data breach legislation should not subject businesses handling the same sensitive customer data to different sets of rules with different penalty regimes, as such a regulatory scheme could lead to inconsistent public notice and enforcement.

Given the breadth of these invasions, if Americans are to be adequately protected and informed, federal legislation to address these threats must cover all of the types of entities that handle sensitive personal information. Exemptions for particular industry sectors not only ignore the scope of the problem, but create risks criminals can exploit. Equally important, a single federal law applying to all breached entities would ensure clear, concise and consistent notices to all affected consumers regardless of where they live or where the breach occurs.

Indeed, Congress could establish the same data breach notice obligations for *all* entities handling sensitive data that suffer a breach of security. Congress should not permit "notice holes" – the situation where certain entities are exempt from reporting known breaches of their own systems. If we want meaningful incentives to increase security, everyone needs to have skin in the game.

Financial Institution Exemptions

Many legislative proposals last Congress, however, had "notice holes," where consumers would not receive disclosures of breaches by certain entities. Perhaps the notice hole that has been left unplugged in most proposals is the exemption from notification standards for entities subject to the Gramm Leach Bliley Act (GLBA), which itself does not contain any statutory language that requires banks to provide notice of their security breaches to affected consumers or the public. Interpretive information security guidelines issued by federal banking regulators in 2005 did not address this lack of a requirement when it set forth an essentially precatory standard for providing consumer notice in the event banks or credit unions were breached. Rather, the 2005 interagency guidelines state that banks and credit unions "should" conduct an investigation to determine whether consumers are at risk due to the breach and, if they determine there is such a risk, they "should" provide consumer notification of the breach.[7] These guidelines fall short of creating a notification requirement using the language of "shall," an imperative command used in proposed breach notification legislation for entities that would be subject to Federal Trade

---

[7] Interagency Guidance on Response Programs for Unauthorized Access to Customer Information and Customer Notice, 70 Fed. Reg. 15736 (Mar. 29, 2005) promulgating 12 C.F.R. Part 30, app. B, Supplement A (OCC); 12 C.F.R. Part 208, app. D-2, Supplement A and Part 225, app. F, Supplement A (Board); 12 C.F.R. Part 364, app. B, Supplement A (FDIC); and 12 C.F.R. Part 570, app. B, Supplement A (OTS), accessible at: https://www.fdic.gov/news/news/financial/2005/fil2705.html.

Commission enforcement. Instead, banks and credit unions are left to make their own determinations about when and whether to inform consumers of a data breach.

Several accounts in 2014 of breaches at the largest U.S. banks demonstrate the lack of any notice requirement under the interagency guidelines. It was reported in news media last fall that as many as one dozen financial institutions were targeted as part of the same cyber-attack scheme.[8] It is not clear to what extent customers of many of those institutions had their data compromised, nor to our knowledge have the identities of all of the affected institutions been made public. The lack of transparency and dearth of information regarding these incidents reflects the fact that banks are not subject to the same requirements to notify affected customers of their own breaches of security as other businesses are required now under 47 state laws and would be required under most proposed federal legislation, despite the fact that financial institutions hold Americans' most sensitive financial information. A number of the more seasoned and robust state laws, such as California's breach notification law, have not exempted financial institutions from their state's breach notification law because they recognize that banks are not subject to any federal requirement that says they "shall" notify customers in the event of a breach of security.

General Principle for Notification

With respect to establishing a national standard for individual notice in the event of a breach of security at an entity handling sensitive personal information, the only principle that makes sense is that these breached entities should be obligated to notify affected individuals or make public notice when they discover breaches of their own systems. Just as the Federal Trade Commission (FTC) expects there to be reasonable data security standards employed by each business that handles sensitive personal information, a federal breach notification bill should apply notification standards that "follow the data" and apply to any entity in a networked system that suffers a breach of security when sensitive data is in its custody. With respect to those who have called upon the entity that is "closest to the consumer" to provide the notice, we would suggest that the one-to-many relationships that exist in the payment card system and elsewhere will ultimately risk having multiple entities all notify about the same breach – someone else's breach. This is not the type of transparent disclosure policy that Congress has typically sought. An effort to promote relevant notices should not obscure transparency as to where a breakdown in the system has occurred. Indeed, a public notice obligation on all entities handling sensitive data would create significant incentives for every business that operates in our networked economy to invest in reasonable data security to protect the sensitive data in its custody. By contrast, a federal law that permits "notice holes" in a networked system of businesses handling the same sensitive personal information – requiring notice of some sectors, while leaving others largely exempt – will unfairly burden the former and unnecessarily betray the public's trust.

Data Security Standards

Data security standards vary depending on the nature of an entity's business and where it operates. Over the past half-century, the United States has essentially taken a sector-specific approach to data privacy (including data security) requirements, and our current legal framework reflects this. For example, credit reporting agencies, financial institutions, and health care

---

[8] "JP Morgan Hackers Said to Probe 13 Financial Firms," *Bloomberg* (Oct. 9, 2014).

providers, just to name a few regulated sectors, have specific data security standards that flow from laws enacted by Congress, such as the Fair Credit Reporting Act (FCRA), the Gramm-Leach-Bliley Act (GLBA), and the Health Insurance Portability and Accountability Act (HIPAA), respectively. Those operating in other industry sectors that are subject to the jurisdiction of the Federal Trade Commission (FTC) must abide by the standards of care enforced by the FTC under Section 5 of the FTC Act, which give the Commission broad, discretionary authority to prosecute "unfair or deceptive acts or practices" (often referred to as their "UDAP" authority). On top of this federal statutory and regulatory framework, states have regulated businesses' data security practices across a variety of industry sectors and enforced consumer protection laws through their state consumer protection agencies and/or their attorneys general.

Legal exposure for data security failures is dependent on the federal or state laws to which a business may be subject and is alleged to violate. The FTC, for example, has been very active in bringing over 50 actions against a range of companies nationwide that are not otherwise subject to a sector-specific federal data security law (e.g., GLBA, HIPAA, etc.). For example, under its Section 5 UDAP authority, the FTC has brought enforcement actions against entities that the Commission believes fall short in providing "reasonable" data security for personal information. Nearly all of these companies have settled with the FTC, paid fines for their alleged violations (sometimes to the extent of millions of dollars), and agreed to raise their security standards and undergo extensive audits of their practices over the next several decades to ensure that their data security standards are in line with the FTC's order.

Effect of Imposing GLBA-Like Standards with FTC Enforcement

In February, 5, 2015, the Senate Commerce Committee held a hearing on data security and breach notification legislation at which NRF testified. Committee Chairman Thune asked of NRF if it was appropriate for GLBA-like data security standards be enforced by the FTC in proposed legislation the committee might consider. We made clear that NRF supports a data security standard, but that federal standards to be enforced by the FTC should be general standards appropriate to the broad array of businesses it would cover. We also noted that it should be enforced consistent with the Commission's long-standing practices under Section 5 of the FTC Act.

Providing the FTC, instead, with the authority to enforce discretionary data security standards like those in the GLBA guidelines would dramatically expand FTC authority. That is because banking regulators take an audit/examination approach to regulating companies and work with them through an iterative process to help the institution come into compliance where it may be lacking, without the threat of severe penalties. The FTC, by contrast, takes an enforcement approach, which under a GLBA guidelines standard, would require a post-hoc determination of a company's compliance with an amorphous standard in a world where the technological threat vectors are ever-changing. In an adversarial investigatory process, like the kind the FTC employs in its enforcement of Section 5, entities are either guilty or not, and more likely to be guilty by the mere fact of a breach. Unlike financial institutions subject to GLBA guidelines, companies subject to FTC enforcement of its UDAP authority are not able to get several bites at the apple working with regulators until they know they are in compliance with the regulator's vision of data security. Rather, businesses facing FTC enforcement would have to guess at what will satisfy the agency and, if their security is breached, the strong enforcement presumption would be that the company failed to meet the subjective standard.

In follow up to the Senate Commerce hearing, NRF sought an expert opinion on the effect of federal legislation that would impose banking industry based data security standards on a vast array of commercial businesses, ranging from large multinational conglomerates to small operations, that are not "financial institutions," including every non-banking business in America that accepts virtually any form of tender (credit cards, debit cards, checks, etc.), other than cash, in exchange for goods and services. As part of your efforts to examine this issue, we strongly encourage you to review the white paper – attached as Appendix A to this testimony – that was prepared by two former associate directors responsible for financial and credit practices in the FTC's Bureau of Consumer Protection and just released on Monday, March 16. The authors' analysis provides a valuable perspective to the Committee and indicates why we believe the broad expansion of data security standards similar to the GLBA guidelines to virtually every unregulated business in the U.S. economy would be a serious error.

Finally, the different enforcement regimes between financial institutions and entities subject to the FTC's jurisdiction is also evident in the manner and frequency with which fines are assessed and civil penalties imposed for non-compliance with a purported data security standard. Banks are rarely (if ever) fined by their regulators for data security weaknesses. But, as noted above, commercial companies have been fined repeatedly by the FTC. Providing an agency like the FTC, with an enforcement approach, a set of standards with significant room for interpretation is likely to lead to punitive actions that are different in kind and effect on entities within the FTC's jurisdiction than the way the standards would be utilized by banking regulators in an examination. A punitive approach to companies already victimized by a crime would not be appropriate nor constructive in light of the fact that the FTC itself has testified before this Committee that no system – even the most protected one money can buy – is ever 100% secure.

Establishing a Nationwide, Uniform Standard of Notification

For more than a decade, the U.S. federalist system has enabled every state to develop its own set of disclosure standards for companies suffering a breach of data security and, to date, 47 states and 4 other federal jurisdictions (including the District of Columbia and Puerto Rico) have enacted varying data breach notification laws. Many of the states have somewhat similar elements in their breach disclosure laws, including definitions of covered entities and covered data, notification triggers, timeliness of notification, provisions specifying the manner and method of notification, and enforcement by state attorneys general. But they do not all include the same requirements, as some cover distinctly different types of data sets, some require that particular state officials be notified, and a few have time constraints (although the vast majority of state laws only require notice "without unreasonable delay" or a similar phrase.)

Over the past ten years, businesses such as retailers, to whom all the state and federal territory disclosure laws have applied, have met the burden of providing notice, even when they did not initially have sufficient information to notify affected individuals, through standardized substitute notification procedures in each state law. However, with an increasingly unwieldy and conflicting patchwork of disclosure laws covering more than 50 U.S. jurisdictions, it is time for Congress to acknowledge that the experimentation in legislation that exists at the state level and that defines our federalist system has reached its breaking point, and it is time for Congress to step in to create a national, uniform standard for data moving in interstate commerce in order to ensure uniformity of a federal act's standards and consistency of their application across jurisdictions.

For years, NRF has called on Congress to enact a preemptive federal breach notification law that is modeled upon the strong consensus of existing laws in nearly every state, the District of Columbia, Puerto Rico and other federal jurisdictions. A single, uniform national standard for notification of consumers affected by a breach of sensitive data would provide simplicity, clarity and certainty to both businesses and consumers alike. Importantly, a single federal law would permit companies victimized by a criminal hacking to devote greater attention in responding to such an attack to securing their networks, determining the scope of affected data, and identifying the customers to be notified, rather than diverting limited time and resources to a legal team attempting to reconcile a patchwork of conflicting disclosure standards in over 50 jurisdictions. In sum, passing a federal breach notification law is a common-sense step that Congress should take now to ensure reasonable and timely notice to consumers while providing clear compliance standards for businesses.

Preemption of state laws and common laws that create differing disclosure standards is never easy, and there is a long history of Supreme Court and other federal courts ruling that, even when Congress expresses an intent to preempt state laws, limiting the scope of the preemption will not result in preemption. All it will accomplish is to add yet another law, this time federal, to the state statutes and common laws already in effect, resulting in the continuation of a confusing tapestry of state law requirements and enforcement regimes. A federal act that leaves this in place would undermine the very purpose and effectiveness of the federal legislation in the first place.

In order to establish a uniform standard, preemptive federal legislation is necessary. But that does not mean (as some have contended) that the federal standard must or should be "weaker" than the state laws it would replace. On the contrary, in return for preemption, the federal law should reflect a strong consensus of the many state laws. Some have called for a more robust notification standard at the federal level than exists at the state level. Without adding unnecessary bells and whistles, NRF believes that Congress can create a stronger breach notification law by removing the exemptions and closing the types of "notice holes" that exist in several state laws, thereby establishing a breach notification standard that applies to all businesses. This approach would enable members that are concerned about preempting state laws to do so with confidence that they have created a more transparent and better notification regime for consumers and businesses alike. It is a way this Congress can work to enact a law with both robust protection and preemption.

We urge Congress, therefore, in pursuing enactment of federal breach notification legislation, to adopt a framework that applies to all entities handling sensitive personal information in order to truly establish uniform, nationwide standards that lead to clear, concise and consistent notices to all affected consumers whenever or wherever a breach occurs. When disclosure standards apply to all businesses that handle sensitive data, it will create the kind of security-maximizing effect that Congress wishes to achieve.

Essential Elements of Data Breach Notification Legislation

In summary, a federal breach notification law should contain three essential elements:

- **Uniform Notice**: Breached entities should be obligated to notify affected individuals or make public notice when they discover breaches of their own systems. A federal law that permits "notice holes" in a networked system of businesses handling the same sensitive personal information – requiring notice of some sectors, while leaving others largely exempt – will unfairly burden the former and unnecessarily betray the public's trust.

- **Express Preemption of State Law**: A single, uniform national standard for notification of consumers affected by a breach of sensitive data would provide simplicity, clarity and certainty to both businesses and consumers alike. Passing a federal breach notification law is a common-sense step that Congress should take now to ensure reasonable and timely notice to consumers while providing clear compliance standards for businesses.

- **Reflect the Strong Consensus of State Laws**: A national standard should reflect the strong consensus of state law provisions. NRF believes that Congress can create a stronger breach notification law by removing the exemptions and closing the types of "notice holes" that exist in several state laws, thereby establishing a breach notification standard that applies to all businesses, similar to the comprehensive approach this Committee has taken in previous consumer protection legislation that is now federal law.

6. Greater Investigation and Prosecution of Cyber Criminals

In addition to the marketplace and technological solutions suggested above, NRF would also support a range of legislative solutions that we believe would help improve the security of our networked systems and ensure better law enforcement tools to address criminal intrusions.

Most important among these legislative solutions would be efforts to strengthen our extra-territorial law enforcement. As noted in our introduction above, industry sectors across the U.S. share the collective concern and face the same threat to their businesses' networks that appear to come predominantly from foreign actors. If the U.S. economy were threatened by foreign actors that had the most sophisticated technology to counterfeit our U.S. dollars, and were using it to perpetrate fraud in the United States and disrupt our economy, would Congress only be asking the victimized companies that accepted counterfeit cash as payment why they did not better protect their customers from this fraud? We think that Congress, in this hypothetical, would look first toward the criminal actors and enterprises that were perpetrating these crimes on our shores. We suggest that this Committee also look abroad to the sources and methods of the cyber attacks that have the same motives and effect as the threats evolve into economic warfare.

We therefore call upon Congress to develop legislation that would provide more tools to law enforcement to ensure that unauthorized network intrusions and other criminal data security breaches – particularly those with foreign attack signatures – are thoroughly investigated and prosecuted, and that the criminals that breach our systems to commit fraud with our customers' information are swiftly brought to justice.

Conclusion

American retailers are targets of cybercrime and suffer approximately 11% of security breaches, predominantly because of the payment card data we accept and process. Criminals desire U.S. based card numbers because they are unprotected and easily sold on the global black market to would-be fraudsters. The data thieves and their criminal customers – the purchasers of these stolen card numbers – realize the short lifespan of stolen card numbers once a breach is detected. This is why the criminals that hack American businesses typically go to extraordinary lengths to mask their incursions with methods that have not been seen before and that are not addressed by network security solutions. In short, if they can act undetected in this "cat-and-mouse" game, and place stolen card numbers on the black market before law enforcement and victimized businesses know the cards are there, they can drive up the market price for the stolen cards.

As stated earlier, retailers have invested billions in adopting data security technology. Efforts to promote payment card security, end-to-end encryption and tokenization are highlighted in our testimony above. The dominant card networks and card-issuing banks, however, have not made all of the technological improvements suggested above to make the payment cards issued in the United States more resistant to fraud, despite the availability of the technology and their adoption of it in many other developed countries of the world, including Canada, the United Kingdom, and most countries of Western Europe. Our ability to improved payment card security and protect American consumers in the chain of the American payment ecosystem is, and will only be, as strong as its weakest link. Without the cooperation of our partners in the financial system, we cannot alone affect the changes necessary to better defend and protect against cyber attacks that lead to payment card fraud. Everyone already has skin in the game, and we need to work together to do what we can to improve an aging and outdated payment system that is the principal target of cyber attacks affecting U.S. retail businesses and their customers.

While everyone in the payments space has a responsibility to do what they can to protect against fraud and data theft that result from cyber attacks, there is much left for card-issuing banks and payment card networks to contribute, as retailers are doing, to better protect our payment system and the fraud-prone cards that are used in them. That is why we have proposed practical, commonsense and achievable solutions above that NRF believes are necessary to helping deter and defend against cyber attacks affecting the retail industry. We appreciate the opportunity to deliver this testimony to the Subcommittee today, and we look forward to working with all the members of the full Committee on bringing greater attention to these issues and helping push forward some or all of our proposed solutions to address these important concerns.

Appendix A:

NRF White Paper on Data Security

(See separate document submitted with testimony)

The Effect of Applying Customer Information Safeguard Requirements for Banks to Nonfinancial Institutions

Joel Winston and Anne Fortney
March 2015

We have been asked to analyze the effect of legislation requiring the Federal Trade Commission ("FTC") to apply standards based upon the Interagency Guidelines for banks in Safeguarding Customer Information ("Interagency Guidelines" or "Guidelines") to any entity that accepts bank-issued payment cards for goods and services and does not extend credit itself.

Summary

The Interagency Guidelines for Safeguarding Customer Information apply to depository institutions ("banks") subject to supervisory examination and oversight by their respective regulatory agencies. The Guidelines contain detailed elements of an information safeguards program tailored specifically to banks. They are designed to be a point of reference in an interactive process between the banks and their examiners, with emphasis on compliance on an on-going basis. The FTC has issued a Safeguards Rule applicable to the nonbank "financial institutions" under its jurisdiction. The Safeguards Rule provides for more flexibility and less specificity in its provisions than do the Guidelines. The more general requirements of the FTC's Rule are designed to be adaptable to ever-changing security threats and to technologies designed to meet those threats.

The differences in the approaches to data security regulation between the Guidelines and the FTC Safeguards Rule reflect two fundamental differences between the bank regulatory agencies (the "Agencies") and the FTC: the substantial differences in the types and sizes of entities within the jurisdiction of the Agencies versus the FTC, and the equally substantial differences in the roles played by the Agencies and the FTC in governing the behavior of those entities. With respect to the former, while the banks covered by the Guidelines are relatively homogeneous, extending the Guidelines to all entities that accept payment cards would sweep in a vast array of businesses ranging from large multinational conglomerates to small operations, and could also include individuals.[1] The threats faced by these widely diverse businesses are likely to vary widely as well, as would the sophistication and capabilities of the entities themselves for addressing the threats. A flexible approach as in the Safeguards Rule is necessary to account for those critical differences. Many of the Guidelines' provisions, which were drafted with banks in mind, likely would be unsuitable for a significant proportion of the entities that would be subject to these new requirements.

---

[1] Because of the near-universal acceptance of bank-issued cards as payment for goods and services, companies that would be subject to the Guidelines' standards would include merchants, hotels, bars and restaurants, theaters, auto dealers, gas stations, grocery and convenience stores, fast-food eateries, airlines and others in the travel industry, hospitals and doctors, dentists, veterinarians, hair salons, gyms, dry cleaners, plumbers and taxi drivers. In other words, virtually all providers of consumer goods and services would be covered.

For similar reasons, the different approaches the Agencies and the FTC take in regulating their entities make it problematic to apply the Guidelines to the nonbank entities overseen by the FTC. The more specific Guidelines make sense when, as is the case with the banks, there is an ongoing, interactive dialogue between the regulated entities and the regulator through the supervision process. The regulated entities and regulators can address changes in threats and technologies during the less formal examination process and head-off potential problems before they happen. By contrast, the Safeguards Rule's flexible requirements are better suited to a law enforcement agency like the FTC that obtains compliance not by an interactive dialogue, but by prosecuting violations after-the-fact. Indeed, an entity within the FTC's jurisdiction may have no indication of deficiencies in its compliance until it is under investigation. With the untold numbers of entities potentially subject to its jurisdiction, the FTC simply lacks the capability or resources to engage in dialogue or provide the individualized, ongoing guidance like the Agencies do with their banks.

While the Guidelines would be made applicable to any entity that accepts bank-issued payment cards,[2] the Guidelines' specific requirements are suitable only for the bank card-issuers that dictate the card processing equipment and procedures for businesses that accept their cards, as well as the security features inherent in the cards. If the Guidelines were made applicable to businesses that merely accept banks' cards, they would impose security obligations on those with the least ability to implement the requirements applicable to payment card security.

Finally, nonbank businesses are subject to the FTC's general authority under the FTC Act to prohibit unfair or deceptive practices, and the FTC has prosecuted many companies under this authority for failing to protect consumer's nonpublic information. Subjecting nonbank businesses to the Guidelines' specific requirements would not enhance the FTC's ability to use its existing authority to protect consumers through enforcement actions. When it issued consumer information privacy and safeguards rules under the Gramm-Leach-Bliley Act, the FTC considered applying the rules to retailers that accept bank credit or debit cards and declined to do so. We believe that determination remains equally justified today.

Our Qualifications

Joel Winston served for 35 years in the FTC's Bureau of Consumer Protection. For nine years, he headed the FTC's offices responsible for consumer information privacy and security, serving as Associate Director for Financial Practices (2000-2005) and for Privacy and Identity Protection (2005-2009). His responsibilities included the development of the FTC Safeguards Rule in 2000-2001, and he directed the FTC's enforcement of that Rule and other consumer protection laws.

---

[2] Bank-issued payment cards include credit cards, debit cards and prepaid cards.

HC# 4847-6208-5922

Anne Fortney has 39 years' experience in the consumer financial services field, including directing FTC enforcement and rulemaking under the federal consumer financial protection laws as the Associate Director for Credit Practices of the Bureau of Consumer Protection.

We both regularly counsel consumer financial services clients on their compliance obligations. We also assist clients in Consumer Financial Protection Bureau ("CFPB") examinations and in the defense of FTC and CFPB investigations and enforcement actions. In addition, we have each testified multiple times as invited witnesses before U.S. Congressional Committees and Subcommittees on various consumer financial protection laws. We each serve from time to time as subject matter experts in litigation in the federal courts involving consumer financial services.

Background

Federal Requirements for Safeguarding Customer Information

Section 501(b) of the Gramm-Leach Bliley Act ("GLBA" or the "Act")[3] required each of the federal bank regulatory agencies (the "Agencies")[4] and the FTC to establish standards for the financial institutions subject to their respective jurisdictions with respect to safeguarding consumers' nonpublic, personal financial information. The Act required that the safeguards ensure the security and confidentiality of customer records and information; protect against any anticipated threats or hazards to the security or integrity of such records; and protect against unauthorized access to or use of such records or information which could result in substantial harm or inconvenience to any customer.[5]

Interagency Guidelines

Because they exercise supervisory responsibilities over banks through periodic examinations, the Agencies issued their GLBA customer information safeguard standards in the form of Guideline document ("Interagency Guidelines" or "Guidelines").[6]

The Guidelines instruct banks on specific factors that serve as the basis for the Agencies' review during supervisory examinations. They are predicated on banks' direct control over the security of their customers' nonpublic personal financial information.

---

[3] Gramm-Leach-Bliley Financial Modernization Act, Pub. L. 106–102, § 501(b) (1999), codified at 15 U.S.C.A. § 6801(b).

[4] These were the Office of the Comptroller of the Currency ("OCC"), the Board of Governors of the Federal Reserve System ("FRB"), the Federal Deposit Insurance Corporation ("FDIC"), and the Office of Thrift Supervision ("OTS"). In October 2011, as a result of the Dodd-Frank Wall Street Reform and Consumer Protection Act, the OTS was terminated and its functions merged into the OCC, FRB, and FDIC.

[5] 15 U.S.C.A. § 6801(b).

[6] Interagency Guidelines Establishing Information Security Standards, 66 Fed. Reg. 8616-01 (Feb. 1, 2001) and 69 Fed. Reg. 77610-01 (Dec. 28, 2004) promulgating and amending 12 C.F.R. Part 30, app. B (OCC); 12 C.F.R. Part 208, app. D-2 and Part 225, app. F (FRB); 12 C.F.R. Part 364, app. B (FDIC); and 12 C.F.R. Part 570, app. B (OTS). The Agencies later issued an interpretive Interagency Guidelines on Response Programs for Unauthorized Access to Customer Information and Customer Notice, 70 Fed. Reg. 15736-01 (Mar. 29, 2005). This paper includes this interpretive Interagency Guidelines in the summary of the Interagency Guidelines.

They instruct each bank to implement a comprehensive written information security program, appropriate to its size and complexity, that: (1) insures the security and confidentiality of consumer information; (2) protects against any anticipated threats or hazards to the security or integrity of such information; and (3) protects against unauthorized access to or use of such information that could result in substantial harm or inconvenience to any customer.

The Guidelines provide specific instructions for banks in the development and implementation of an information security program. A bank must:

- Involve the Board of Directors, which must approve the information security program and oversee the development, implementation and maintenance of the program;
- Assess risk, including reasonably foreseeable internal and external threats, the likelihood and potential damage of these threats, and the sufficiency of the bank's policies and procedures in place to control risk;
- Design the program to control identified risks. Each bank must consider whether the following security measures are appropriate for the bank, and, if so, adopt the measures it concludes are appropriate:
    - Access controls on customer information systems;
    - Access restrictions at physical locations containing customer information;
    - Encryption of electronic customer information;
    - Procedures designed to ensure that customer information system modifications are consistent with the bank's information security program;
    - Dual control procedures,
    - Segregation of duties, and employee background checks for employees responsible for customer information;
    - Response programs that specify actions to be taken when the bank suspects or detects unauthorized access to customer information systems, including appropriate reports to regulatory and law enforcement agencies; and
    - Measures to protect against destruction, loss, or damage of customer information due to potential environmental hazards;
- Train staff to implement the information security program;
- Regularly test key controls, systems, and procedures of the information security program;
- Develop, implement, and maintain appropriate measures to properly dispose of customer information and consumer information;
- Adequately oversee service provider arrangements, including by contractually requiring service providers to implement appropriate procedures and monitoring service providers;
- Adjust the program in light of relevant changes in technology, sensitivity of consumer information, internal and external threats, the bank's own changing business arrangements, and changes to customer information systems;
- Report to the Board of Directors at least annually; and

- Provide for responses to data breaches involving sensitive customer information,[7] which should include –
  - Developing a response program as a key part of its information security program, which includes, at a minimum, procedures for assessing the nature and scope of an incident;
  - Notifying the bank's primary federal regulator as soon as the bank becomes aware of the breach;
  - Notifying appropriate law enforcement authorities;
  - Containing and controlling the incident to prevent further unauthorized access to or use of consumer information; and
  - Notifying consumers of a breach when the bank becomes aware of an incident of unauthorized access to sensitive customer information. The notice must include certain content and must be given in a clear and conspicuous manner and delivered in any manner designed to ensure the customer can reasonably be expected to receive it.

FTC Safeguards Rule[8]

The FTC protects consumers against "unfair and deceptive acts and practices in or affecting commerce."[9] Its jurisdiction includes "all persons, partnerships, or corporations," except banks, savings and loan institutions, federal credit unions and certain nonfinancial entities regulated by other federal agencies.[10] The FTC issues substantive rules, such as the Safeguards Rule, when required by Congress to do so,[11] but it is not authorized to conduct supervisory examinations of entities under its broad jurisdiction. Rather, the FTC is primarily a law enforcement agency.

Because the FTC lacks supervisory examination authority, it issued a Safeguards Rule, rather than Guidelines, to establish customer information safeguards for "financial institutions" under its jurisdiction. The GLBA's broad definition of "financial institution" includes a myriad of nonbank companies that operate in the consumer financial services industry.[12] The definition includes finance companies, auto dealers, debt collectors and consumer reporting agencies,

---

[7] Sensitive customer information includes: a customer's name, address, or telephone number, in conjunction with the customer's social security number, driver's license number, account number, credit or debit card number, or a personal identification number or password that would permit access to the customer's account, and any combination of components of customer information that would allow someone to log onto or access the customer's account (i.e., user name and password, or password and account number). 12 C.F.R. Part 30, app. B, supp. A, § III.A.1; 12 C.F.R. Part 208, app. D-2, supp. A, § III.A.1, and Part 225, app. F, supp. A, § III.A.1; 12 C.F.R. Part 364, app. B, supp. A, § III.A.1; and 12 C.F.R. Part 570, app. B, supp. A, § III.A.1.

[8] FTC Safeguards Rule, 16 CFR Part 314. The FTC issued the final rule in 2001.

[9] 15 U.S.C.A. § 45(a)(1). The FTC Act also prohibits unfair methods of competition in or affecting commerce.

[10] 15 U.S.C.A. § 45(a)(2). For example, the FTC Act exempts not-for-profit entities and common carriers subject to the Communications Act of 1934.

[9] The FTC has more general rulemaking authority under Section 18 of the FTC Act, 15 U.S.C.A. § 57a, but has promulgated very few rules under that section in recent years.

[12] See 15 U.S.C.A. § 6809(3) (defining "financial institution" to include any institution engaging in "financial activities"); 12 U.S.C.A. § 1843(k) (defining "financial activities" broadly to include activities that are "financial in nature or incidental to such financial activity" or "complementary to a financial activity").

among many others. The FTC determined that the final Rule would not apply to retailers that merely accept payment cards, but rather only to those that extend credit themselves, and only then to the extent of their credit granting activities.[13]

In recognition of the great variety of businesses covered by the Safeguards Rule, the FTC developed a rule that provided for flexible safeguard procedures that could be adapted to the myriad ways in which covered entities are structured and operate. The FTC Rule requires a financial institution to develop, implement, and maintain a comprehensive written information security program that contains safeguards that are appropriate to the entity's size and complexity, the nature and scope of its activities, the types of risks it faces, and the sensitivity of the customer information it collects and maintains. The information security program must: (1) ensure the security and confidentiality of consumer information; (2) protect against any anticipated threats or hazards to the security or integrity of such information; and (3) protect against unauthorized access to or use of such information that could result in substantial harm or inconvenience to any customer.

In its development, implementation, and maintenance of the information security program, the financial institution must:

- Designate an employee or employees to coordinate the program;
- Identify reasonably foreseeable internal and external risks to data security and assess the sufficiency of safeguards in place to control those risks in each relevant area of the financial institution's operations (i.e., employee training, information systems, prevention/response measures for attacks);
- For all relevant areas of the institution's operations, design and implement information safeguards to control the risks identified in the risk assessment, and regularly test and monitor the effectiveness of key controls, systems, and procedures;
- Oversee service providers, including by requiring service providers to implement and maintain safeguards for customer information; and
- Evaluate and adjust the program in light of material changes to the institution's business that may affect its safeguards.

---

[13] *See* 16 C.F.R. §§ 314.2(a) (adopting the Privacy Rule's definition of "financial institution"). That definition includes examples of "financial institutions," among them: retailers that extend credit by issuing their own credit cards directly to consumers; businesses that print and sell checks for consumers; businesses that regularly wire money to and from consumers; check cashing businesses; accountants; real estate settlement service providers; mortgage brokers; and investment advisors 16 C.F.R. § 313.3(k)(2). The FTC also opined that debt collectors are "financial institutions." 65 Fed Reg. 33646; 33655 (May 24, 2000). Further, the Privacy Rule also gives examples of entities that are *not* "financial institutions": retailers that only extend credit via occasional "lay away" and deferred payment plans or accept payment by means of credit cards issued by others; retailers that accept payment in the form of cash, checks, or credit cards that the retailer did not issue; merchants that allow customers to "run a tab"; and grocery stores that allow customers to cash a check or write a check for a higher amount than the grocery purchase and obtain cash in return. *Id.* at (k)(3).

When it promulgated this rule, the FTC considered requiring more specific and detailed data security requirements, but determined that doing so would have imposed significant regulatory burdens in light of the broad range of entities potentially subject to the Safeguards Rule.

Comparison of the Interagency Guidelines and the FTC Rule

Both the Interagency Guidelines and the FTC Rule apply only to "financial institutions" with respect to the "nonpublic personal" financial information they collect and maintain. Unlike the Guidelines, however, the FTC Rule applies to many types of entities whose principal business may not involve the provision of financial services to consumers.

While the Guidelines and the FTC Rule share some common elements, they differ in critical respects. In particular, the Interagency Guidelines, which are tailored to closely supervised and regulated banks, are much more detailed in their requirements. These requirements are designed to be the point of reference in an interactive process between the banks and their examiners. As their name implies, the Guidelines are intended to guide banks' compliance on a going forward basis.

In contrast, the FTC Rule is significantly less specific in its data security requirements than the Guidelines, because the Rule applies to a much broader and more diverse group of entities with wider variations in the data they collect and maintain, the risks they face, and the tools they have available to address those risks. The more general requirements of the FTC Rule also are designed to be adaptable to the near-constant changes in threats, security technologies, and other evolutionary developments in this extremely dynamic area. Whereas the Agencies can address new developments through the interactive examination process, the FTC only has the blunt instrument of law enforcement. And, whereas the Agencies actively supervise and monitor the activities of the entities they oversee, the FTC can only investigate and, if appropriate, take enforcement action against a fraction of the entities over which it has jurisdiction. The FTC's primary focus is on prosecuting past or existing deficiencies, and a company may receive no advance warning of a possible violation of the Safeguards Rule until it is confronted with an adversarial investigation. The Agencies' goal, on the other hand, is to prevent future deficiencies by working with the bank on an ongoing basis.

Effect of an FTC Standard That Would Apply Interagency Guidelines to Nonbanks That Do Not Extend Credit and Only Accept Credit Cards

For several reasons, safeguards requirements designed for closely supervised banks that issue credit and debit cards are a poor fit for the vast array of entities that accept credit cards and debit cards as payment for their goods and services. First, as explained above, the Guidelines are premised on an ongoing and interactive process between regulator and regulated entity, whereby examiners can instruct a bank on an apparent failure to meet a specific requirement. This process enables the institution to explain why a particular element of the Guidelines may be inapplicable or to correct any real deficiencies without legal sanctions.

No such process is possible for entities subject to FTC oversight. The FTC obtains compliance by initiating law enforcement investigations, using compulsory process, when it suspects a potential law violation based on facts that have come to its attention. This "after the fact" review focuses, through an adversarial process, on the legal requirements or prohibitions that may have been violated. If violations are found, the FTC seeks a formal order prohibiting the illegal conduct and, in appropriate cases, imposing fines or redress to injured consumers. The FTC lacks supervisory examination authority and lacks the resources to provide the specific guidance and ongoing oversight that would be necessary to effectuate Guidelines-type rules covering the huge diversity of nonbank entities. The result would be comparable to the widespread confusion and noncompliance that resulted from the FTC's attempt to so broadly define "creditors" subject to its Red Flags Rule[14] that the Rule would apply to types of businesses (such as plumbers, dry cleaners, hospitals, and restaurants) for which the Rule requirements made little sense. Congress had to correct that result with legislation that "reined in" the FTC by limiting the rule to the kinds of "creditors" that need written procedures to detect and prevent identity theft, rather than virtually every consumer-facing business.[15]

Second, many of the specific requirements of the Guidelines simply are not relevant to, or would impose unreasonable obligations on, nonbanks. For example, with respect to credit and debit cards, the Guidelines' obligations are premised on the specific circumstances and capabilities of card *issuers*, which differ substantially from those of entities that accept cards as payment. It is the card issuers, and not the card-accepting merchants, be they hotels or veterinarians, that dictate the card processing capabilities of the equipment and procedures that merchants must use, as well as the security features inherent in the cards. Although chip and PIN technology could reduce card fraud, and many retailers have demonstrated a willingness to install terminals to accept cards with that technology, only card-issuing financial institutions can decide whether to issue fraud-resistant chip and PIN cards. Were the FTC required to enforce safeguard standards for credit and debit card data based on the Guidelines' model, it would be imposing obligations on the entities with the least ability to ensure that they were carried out.

Finally, it is important to note that nonbanks, although not covered by the Safeguards Rule, are subject to the FTC's general authority under Section 5 of the FTC Act to prohibit unfair or deceptive practices. The FTC has used this authority to prosecute dozens of nonbanks for engaging in the same practices proscribed by the Safeguards Rule, i.e., failing to take reasonable measures to protect consumers' personally identifiable information.[16] Thus, it is unclear what

---

[14] *See* 16 C.F.R. Parts 681.1(b)(4), (5) (2009) (effective until February 11, 2013) (referring to 15 U.S.C.A. § 1691a(r)(5) (the Equal Credit Opportunity Act), which defines "creditor" as, among other things, "any person who regularly extends, renews, or continues credit," and defines "credit" as "the right granted by a creditor to a debtor to... *purchase property or services and defer payment therefor*") (emphasis added).

[15] Red Flag Program Clarification Act of 2010, Pub. L. 111-319, § 2 (2010).

[16] *See, e.g., FTC v. Wyndham Worldwide Corp., et al.*, No. CV 12-1365-PHXPGR, in the U.S. District Court for the District of Arizona (2012); *In the Matter of Fandango, LLC*, Matter Number 132 3089 (2014); *In the Matter of Cbr Systems, Inc.*, Matter Number: 112 3120 (2013); *In the Matter of Dave & Buster's Inc.*, Matter Number 082 3153

additional benefit to the public would gain by subjecting nonbanks to specific requirements of the Guidelines.

As noted earlier, when issuing the GLBA rules, including the Safeguards Rule, the FTC specifically considered whether the rules should apply to retailers that accept bank-issued credit cards but do not extend credit themselves. The FTC correctly concluded that to do so would constitute a significant expansion of the FTC's authority to encompass the regulation of any transaction involving acceptance of a payment, whether cash, cards, checks or otherwise.

(2010); *In the Matter of CVS Caremark Corp.*, Matter Number: 072-3119 (2009); *In the Matter of Gencia Corp. and Compgeeks.com d/b/a computer Geeks Discount Outlet and Geeks.com*, Matter Number: 082 3113 (2009); *In the Matter of TJX Companies*, Matter Number: 072-3055 (2008); *In the Matter of Life is good, Inc. and Life is good Retail, Inc.*, Matter Number: 0723046 (2008); *U.S. v. ValueClick, Inc., et al.*, No. CV 08-01711, in the U.S. District Court for the Central District of California (2008); *In the Matter of Guidelines Software, Inc.*, Matter Number: 062 3057 (2007); *In the Matter of CardSystems Solutions, Inc.*, Matter Number: 052 3148 (2006); *In the Matter of DSW Inc.*, Matter Number: 052 3096 (2006); *In the Matter of BJ's Wholesale Club, Inc.*, Matter Number: 042 3160 (2005); *In the Matter of Petco Animal Supplies, Inc.*, Matter Number: 0323221 (2005); *In the Matter of Guess?, Inc. and Guess.com, Inc.*, Matter Number: 022 3260 (2003). These actions are in addition to those that the FTC has brought under the GLBA Safeguards Rule and/or the Consumer Information Disposal Rule. *See, e.g., U.S. v. PLS Financial Services, Inc., et al.*, Case No. 1:12-cv-08334, in the U.S. District Court for the Northern District of Illinois, Eastern Division (2012); *In the Matter of James B. Nutter & Company*, Matter Number: 0723108 (2009); *In the Matter of Premier Capital Lending*, Matter Number: 072 3004 (2008); *U.S. v. American United Mortgage Co.*, Civil Action No. 07C 7064, in the U.S. District Court for the Northern District of Illinois, Eastern Division (2007); *In the Matter of Nations Title Agency, Inc., et al.*, Matter Number: 052 3117 (2006).

Appendix B:

What Retailers Want You To Know About Data Security[9]

---

[9] Slides Available at: http://www.slideshare.net/NationalRetailFederation/thingsto-know-datasecurity?ref=https://nrf.com/media/press-releases/retailers-reiterate-support-federal-data-breach-notification-standard

What retailers want you to know about.....

DATA SECURITY

NRF RETAIL

BREAKDOWN

What is a data breach?

A data breach is the unauthorized acquisition of sensitive personal information in digital, electronic or computerized form that creates a risk of financial harm to a consumer.

NRF RETAIL

Who is breaching?

Cybercriminals are constantly trolling for financial data in order to steal card numbers and convert them into cash.

NRF RETAIL

Where do breaches happen?

Hackers don't discriminate – data breaches have targeted a wide variety of businesses from the entertainment industry to financial services.

According to Verizon, retail represents 11 percent of data breaches while the financial services industry accounts for 34 percent.

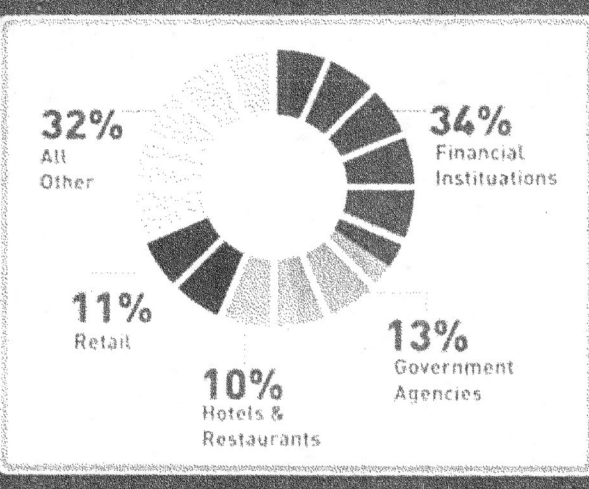

32% All Other

34% Financial Institutions

11% Retail

10% Hotels & Restaurants

13% Government Agencies

NRF RETAIL

ABOUT

Why retailers care about data security.

As a consumer-facing and reliant industry, retailers and merchants value every interaction with their customers.

Retailers work every single day and make significant contributions and investments in data, information and payment security to ensure that the retail-customer relationship is secure and protected.

NRF RETAIL

PROBLEM

Cards are fraud prone

The thief creates a duplicate card, signs your name and makes a purchase.

The thief uses your card, signs your name and makes a purchase.

NRF RETAIL

49

PIN-and-Chip

SOLUTION

Since 2005, the National Retail Federation has urged banks and payment card companies to switch to more secure PIN-and-chip cards, which replace the magnetic stripe with a computer microchip and replace the signature with a Personal Identification Number(PIN) to better protect consumers' financial data when they shop.

The new credit cards being issued this year need to have both a chip and a PIN, not just a chip as proposed by most banks and credit unions. The chip ensures that the card is the one issued by the bank but the PIN is needed to ensure that the person using the card is the actual cardholder and not a thief who stole your chip card.

SOLUTION

PIN and CHIP

Only you know your PIN, so the thief can't enter it to complete an in-store transaction.

The thief cannot duplicate your chip card.

MAGNETIC STRIPE and SIGNATURE

The thief uses your card, signs your name, and makes a purchase.

The thief creates a duplicate card, signs your name, and makes a purchase.

YOUR CARD IS STOLEN

YOUR CARD INFO IS STOLEN

The safest cards deploy both PIN and Chip technology.

PIN and Chip is widely used around the world with great success; the United Kingdom saw a 75% drop in credit card fraud after implementation.

American consumers deserve better.

PROBLEM

Cyber-Threat Information Sharing

Congress must pass laws that make it easier for companies to share information and emerging threats without hesitation.

SOLUTION

NRF's Efforts to Improve Threat Information Sharing

To help fight cybersecurity threats to retailers' systems, NRF created the Information Technology Security Council, which keeps retailers up-to-date on the latest news, information and threats. More than 150 retail companies are actively involved.

Notification isn't uniform

PROBLEM

For the past decade, NRF has called for a uniform nationwide data breach notification standard that would preempt the patchwork of 47 state laws. This uniform federal law should be based on and reflect the strong consensus of state laws.

The current patchwork of state and local data breach notice laws with conflicting requirements doesn't work because it diverts limited resources that should be focused on restoring the integrity of a breached system.

NRF RETAIL

Data Breach Notification Law

SOLUTION

A nationwide breach notification law must preempt state and local laws so businesses and consumers understand what disclosures are expected regardless of when or where breaches occur.

Data breach notification should be appropriate, reasonable, relevant and timely.

Federal data breach notification requirements should be comprehensive and apply to every entity that maintains or transmits sensitive information, not just retailers.

NRF RETAIL

Industries are held to different standards

Merchants have multiple tiers of data security standards. These include Payment Card Industry standards for all merchants accepting payment cards, as well as specific state standards to protect sensitive information. The Federal Trade Commission also enforces federal standards that require all merchants to have reasonable data security protections.

Other breached entities just need to follow industry-specific guidance.

NRF RETAIL

Cover all entities involved in data breach

A data breach notification law should cover the entire payments system from card companies to telecommunications firms without exception or exemption. Arbitrary timeframes or industry-specific requirements that cover only certain entities should not be established.

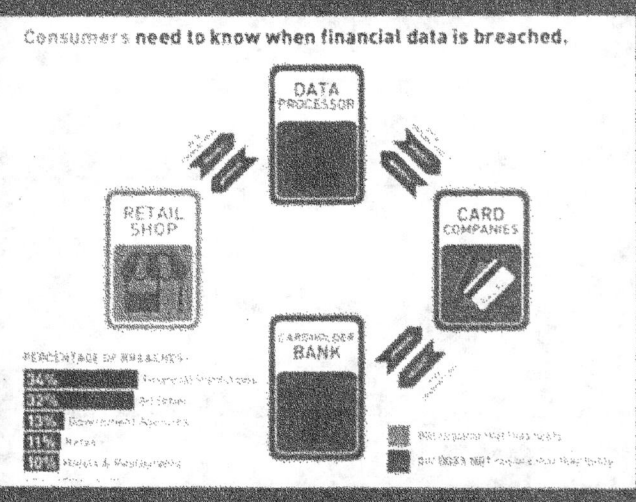

Consumers need to know when financial data is breached.

NRF RETAIL

Mr. HURD. Thank you, Mr. French.

Mr. Nutkis?

STATEMENT OF DANIEL NUTKIS

Mr. NUTKIS. Good afternoon, Chairman Hurd and Ranking Member Kelly. It is a pleasure to join the subcommittee this afternoon to share HITRUST's perspective on the cyber threats facing the health care industry.

While I prepared my written Statement for the record, I would like to share with you a few key points.

Health Information Trust Alliance was formed in 2007 with the singular mission to streamline the safeguarding of sensitive information systems and devices in use within the health care system.

Our perspective on the evolving cyber security threats facing the health care industry is formed based on our deep engagement with industry around information protection. That engagement includes data from over 10,000 security assessments done in 2014 alone, leveraging the HITRUST CSF.

The HITRUST CSF is a scalable prescriptive and certifiable risk-based framework developed for and with the health care industry, incorporating relevant NIST, ISAO, PCI and other standards, supports various Federal and State regulations like HIPPA and HP300 in Texas, incorporates best practices and lessons learned including analysis of breached data, incorporates 135 security controls and 14 privacy controls. It was first released in 2008 and is currently on Version 7.

It should also be noted that we identified security controls relevant to cyber threats prior to the release of the NIST cyber security framework which is now fully mapped into the HITRUST CSF.

It should also be noted that approximately 85 percent adoption by hospitals and health plans make it the most widely adopted in the industry.

Also influencing our perspective is the HITRUST Cyber Threat Intelligence and Incident Coordination Center, C3, which is the most active cyber center in health care established in 2012. It is a federally recognized ISAO or information sharing and analysis organization.

It supports threat intelligence sharing and incident coordination for the health care industry. It includes threat sharing with the Department of Health and Human Services and Homeland Security. It has four key components.

The Cyber Threat XChange, CTX, was created to accelerate the sharing, distribution and consumption of threat indicators. It has been noted that the CTX is a revamp of a process that failed, in this case providing indicators of compromise in electronic consumer format such as STIX, TAXII and proprietary SIEM formats, streamlining the process of making information more consumable. We make that available free of charge.

The second component is something called Health Care CyberVision which was created to enhance awareness of unknown threats, provide early warning or a more perspective view into the unknown cyber threat environment which provides situational awareness by testing the effectiveness of security defenses against emerging and unknown threats.

The third component is something we call CyberRx which is in its second year, which is a series of cyber preparedness and response exercises to simulate cyber attacks on health care organizations. We expanded that significantly this year to include a much larger part of the industry.

The fourth component is our cyber monthly threat briefings. Every month, HITRUST, in conjunction with the Department of Health and Human Services hosts a cyber threat briefing to help raise awareness and educate the industry relating to cyber threats.

Our familiarity in engaging with industry affords us certain insights into cyber preparedness, risk management and cyber risk indicators that have the potential to impact privacy, disrupt facility operations or cause direct harm to patients.

We have information protection maturity in organization with over 400,000 organizations ranging from Fortune 15 to solo practitioners. We have a wide range of information security sophistication which significantly complicates the detection sharing and response of any solution or approach. More needs to be done to ensure we are addressing the real needs of the market.

Many organizations do not understand the cyber threats and risks relevant to their organization and spend unnecessary and limited resources in tracking down things that are not relevant.

We need to look more at high tech, low touch approaches to automate more of the process and make it more actionable for a wider range of organizations.

As to specific motives, many health care organizations are a treasure trove for threat actors. They store or process IP, EII, DII, DHI, financial information, medical information and much of it fully linked together. This makes the industry a high value target.

The other panelists already mentioned threat actors. It is a wide range of actors from nations, States to hackers of opportunity.

A health plan was most recently a target of choice given the magnitude and breadth of information they possess. Hospitals face unique threats given their position of providing care directly to patients and their position of procuring and implementing medical devices and new technologies in their infrastructure.

I do not make these statements lightly with the intention of causing undue harm. As I said before, health care is a high value and target rich environment. We have come a long way but still have a long journey ahead of us.

With that, Mr. Chairman, I am pleased to answer the committee's questions.

[Prepared Statement of Mr. Nutkis follows:]

Testimony of Dan Nutkis
CEO of HITRUST Alliance

Before the Oversight and Government Reform Committee,
Subcommittee on Information Technology

Hearing entitled: "Cybersecurity: The Evolving Nature of Cyber Threats
Facing the Private Sector"
March 18, 2015

Prepared for Submission

Chairman Hurd, Ranking Member Kelly, and distinguished Members of the
Subcommittee, I am pleased to appear today to discuss the role HITRUST plays to
address persistent and emerging cyber threats to healthcare. I am Daniel Nutkis,
CEO and founder of the Health Information Trust Alliance or HITRUST. I
founded HITRUST in 2007, after recognizing the need to formally and
collaboratively address information security for healthcare stakeholders from all
segments of industry, insurers, providers, pharmacies, PBMs and manufacturers.
HITRUST endeavored to elevate the level of information protection in the
healthcare industry—ensuring greater collaboration between industry and
government, and raising the competency level of information security
professionals.

With regards to aiding industry in cyber risk management, threat preparedness and
response, HITRUST has implemented numerous programs in coordination with
industry stakeholders. The HITRUST CSF, is a scalable, prescriptive and
certifiable risk-based framework relating to information security tailored to the
healthcare industry. Over 84 percent of hospitals and health plans, as well as many
other healthcare organizations and business associates, have adopted the CSF,
making it the most widely adopted security framework in healthcare.

In 2008 and five years prior to the issuance of Executive Order (EO) 13636,
"Improving Critical Infrastructure Cybersecurity" issued by the President on
February 12, 2013 and before the NIST published its Cyber Security Framework,
HITRUST published the first volume of the CSF and had already identified
information protection controls relating to cyber security and issued guidance to
the healthcare industry. The CSF is continuously updated to ensure relevance, such
as incorporating the NIST Cyber Security Framework and providing health
industry implementation guidance as well as privacy controls.

The HITRUST CSF Assurance Program delivers simplified compliance assessment and reporting for HIPAA, HITECH, state, and business associate requirements. Leveraging the CSF, the program provides healthcare organizations and their business associates with a common approach to manage security assessments that creates efficiencies and contains costs associated with multiple and varied assurance requirements. The CSF Assurance Program includes the risk management oversight and assessment methodology governed by HITRUST and designed for the unique regulatory and business needs of the healthcare industry.

Additionally, MyCSF is a full-featured, user-friendly, fully-integrated and managed tool that streamlines the entire information compliance and risk management process, from policy creation, approval and publication to risk assessment and remediation. The optimized and powerful tool marries the content and methodologies of the CSF and CSF Assurance Program with the technology and capabilities of a governance, risk and compliance (GRC) tool.

In 2012, after identifying the need for coordination among stakeholders, particularly leveraging the expertise of more cyber-sophisticated organizations to assist less sophisticated players, HITRUST launched the Cyber Threat Intelligence and Incident Coordination Center (C^3) to provide threat intelligence, coordinated incident response and knowledge transfer specific to cyber threats pertinent to the healthcare industry. The C^3 facilitates the early identification of cyber-attacks and creation of best practices specific to the healthcare environment and maintains a conduit through the Department of Homeland Security (DHS) to the broader cyber-intelligence community for analysis support and exchange of threat intelligence. The Center was also the first to track vulnerabilities related to medical devices and electronic health record systems, which are both emerging areas of concern.

The HITRUST Cyber Threat XChange (CTX) was created to significantly accelerate the detection of and response to cyber threat indicators targeted at the healthcare industry. HITRUST CTX automates the process of collecting and analyzing cyber threats and distributing actionable indicators in electronically consumable formats (e.g. STIX, TAXII and proprietary SIEM formats) that organizations of almost all sizes and cyber security maturity can utilize to improve their cyber defenses. HITRUST CTX will act as an advanced early warning system as cyber threats are perpetrated on the industry. CTX is now offered free of charge to the public and has gained wide acceptance within healthcare.

Additionally, HITRUST developed CyberRX, now in its second year, which is a series of industry-wide exercises developed by HITRUST and the Department of Health and Human Services (HHS), to simulate cyber-attacks on healthcare organizations in order to evaluate the industry's response and threat preparedness against attacks and attempts to disrupt U.S. healthcare industry operations. These exercises examine both broad and segment-specific scenarios targeting information systems, medical devices, and other essential technology resources of the Health and Public Health Sector. CyberRX findings are analyzed and used to identify areas for improvement for industry, government and HITRUST C^3 and understand what improvements are needed to enhance information sharing between healthcare organizations, C^3, and government agencies.

Finally, HITRUST and HHS coordinate a monthly Health Industry Monthly Cyber Threat Briefing – which is open to the public – that provides timely insights on emerging cyber threats and countermeasures. HITRUST is also an active participant on the Health Sector Coordinating Council (SCC) and provides a monthly cyber threat briefings to the SCC.

HITRUST is also a federally recognized information sharing and analysis organization (ISAO), has strong relationships with HHS, DHS and the Federal Bureau of Investigation (FBI) and considers them integral partners to elevate the threat landscape facing healthcare today and strengthen the continuum of care.

In my testimony today, I would like to highlight how HITRUST helps elevate the cyber awareness, preparedness and response of the healthcare industry. Growing cyber threats are an increasing risk to not just all areas of critical infrastructure; but healthcare specifically. Increasingly, private sector networks are experiencing nation-state cyber activity similar to that seen on Federal networks. In addition to targeting government networks, there is a growing threat of nation-states targeting and compromising critical infrastructure networks and systems. Healthcare is no exception and is not immune from such threats.

Mitigating the risks associated with cyber threats and attacks requires a comprehensive approach including implementing strong security controls, monitoring control effectiveness, and testing preparedness and response. Commonly applied, "network hygiene" only covers the blocking and tackling. While there is not a perfect solution to information security; the best strategy is to prevent, detect and respond, before the adversary achieves his objective. Strategically, information sharing is designed to assist with this; however, information sharing is a predominantly reactive approach and also dependent on the maturity of the industry. Since this is something we have been struggling with in healthcare, HITRUST is exploring new approachs to take information sharing to the next level by identifying the exploits that are "in the wild" and tracking how they are impact applications and implemented security products. We have named our new approach, CyberVision. While it is in the pilot stage, it is gaining increased attention and we look forward to the opportunity to continue to update the Committee on our progress.

We believe an approach like CyberVision transforms cyber risk management and is so important at this stage because we need to move all areas of critical infrastructure from a posture of being reactive to proactive. If healthcare can inform the overall proactive information sharing approach then we are eager to tackle this challenge head on. While threat intelligence can help defenders more quickly identify and respond to intrusions, this information only helps if the organization is postured to succeed. Until one invests in sound strategy, processes, people and technology, no amount of information sharing or threat intelligence will be sufficient. CyberVision is one way HITRUST is elevating the strategy, people and technology so that organizations can focus their resources where it counts.

Since 2007, HITRUST has endeavored to elevate the level of information protection by ensuring greater collaboration between industry and government, and raising the competency level of information security professionals across the healthcare industry. We have tremendous experience as a federally recognized ISAO and have many valuable lessons to share. In the past, there has been some confusion on who in the private sector companies can turn to in order to work with their government partners. HITRUST is determined to be the focal link that will continue to provide value to strengthen our government, our economy, and our nation as a whole given the growing cyber threats the nation faces.

HITRUST, as the healthcare industry's largest and leading ISAO, has taken a holistic approach to threat intelligence sharing and cybersecurity from the beginning with the HITRUST C3 program, the CTX, the Monthly Threat Briefings, and the CyberRX attack simulation exercises. HITRUST is also a leader in education and outreach. HITRUST's CSF incorporates the NIST cyber security framework to ensure the CSF is the healthcare sector's premier framework and also an example for other sectors given its rigorous privacy controls.

In the wake of the recent Anthem breach, the industry was able to experience the effectiveness of information sharing as HITRUST was able to share Indicators of Compromise (IOCs) with the healthcare industry within one hour after Anthem posted them to the HITRUST CTX. In addition they were shared with HHS, DHS and U.S. CERT who shared the IOCs with other industry ISAOs.

In conclusion, I would like to discuss several challenges the industry faces. There is certainly a maturity problem in every industry but especially in healthcare. The industry struggles with the fact that regulators do not acknowledge companies that invest and demonstrate security maturity above the industry standard. Specifically, industry is seeking ways to demonstrate that such investments receive appropriate recognition and provide safe harbor from regulators and claims of negligence. We would like such efforts and evidence of program effectiveness to be accepted by regulators including the HHS's Office of Civil Rights and the Federal Trade Commission. The CSF is one such area of effectiveness that has wide industry support and adoption.

The industry seeks to be at the forefront of intelligence sharing and cyber collaboration with the Federal Government. Evidence gathered from the CTX and other threat streams demonstrate the growing interest in our industry by nation-state actors which introduces attack scenarios that even the best companies will have a difficult time preventing. The standard needed to resist such efforts is perfection which is very difficult to sustain. Our industry is required to maintain some of the most sensitive information available on Americans. Each dollar spent responding to an attack siphons money from the healthcare delivery system of our country. Consumer confidence is a critical component of our ability to electronically engage consumers in proactive health management and disease intervention measures. Fear of engaging with the health system can only impact the well-being of our population over time. HITRUST, through its many tools and programs seeks to ensure that the healthcare system can properly address this challenge and we stand as a leader in this endeavor.

Thank you again for the opportunity to join you today and share these insights. I look forward to your questions.

Mr. HURD. Thank you very much, Mr. Nutkis.
Mr. JOHNSON.

STATEMENT OF DOUG JOHNSON

Mr. JOHNSON. Chairman Hurd, Ranking Member Kelly and members of the subcommittee, my name is Doug Johnson. I am Senior Vice President and Chief Advisor, Payments and Cybersecurity Policy at the American Bankers Association.

I really do appreciate the opportunity to be here today and discuss cyber security as well as representing the ABA. I am also the Vice Chairman of the Financial Services Sector Coordinating Council and on the board of the Financial Service Information Sharing and Analysis Center.

The Council has been in operation since 2002. The ISAC has been in operation since 1999. We are fairly mature in terms of our approach to these issues. I really do appreciate having the opportunity to provide the perspectives we have developed over the years.

As the 114th Congress engages in public debate on the important issue of cyber security, we share your concerns regarding the evolving nature of the threats. We certainly do support effective cyber security policy. We want to continue to work with Congress toward that.

I will focus on three main points: the evolving nature of cyber threats, the role of technology in addressing those threats and the role of expanded information sharing in protecting against the threats as well I think is very important.

One thing that is evidence is that attacks used to be very singular in focus, be it a denial of service attack against a financial institution, an attack against a merchant's point of sale device or maybe an attempt to destroy or wipe data of an energy company like Saudi ARAMCO.

I think what we see now is sort of blended attacks where these multifaceted attacks create particular challenges for us because essentially they necessitate a simultaneous maintenance of availability integrity and confidentiality of data where formerly a cyber security attack would maybe have the impact on one of those data components.

That creates some resource constraints in some instances when you are trying to respond to those incidents.

We are also seeing is attackers of every variety are becoming increasingly adept at defeating security practices. We have seen the velocity increase with which companies must move so they can ensure they understand how the cyber risks are changing and mitigating measures most effective against those risks. It is an arms race. Indeed, it really is an arms race.

Another increased challenge for institutions and the private sector—Mr. Nutkis alluded to this—is essentially the voluminous nature of the threat data which we have now. It is not as readily consumable as it could be.

Determining the relevance of a particular piece of threat data, analyzing the magnitude of the threat, evaluating which systems might be impacted and devising the appropriate course to take in mitigating against the threat is becoming increasingly difficult to accomplish. I will touch on that when we talk about information sharing.

Last, the victim of the attack is also changing. Prior to 2014, much of the private and public sector energy was focused on critical infrastructure and payments. I think what we have seen based on 2014 is a recognition that there is a broader motivation for attackers in conducting a cyber attack. Essentially any company in any sector could be subject to a significant and highly visible attack.

Technology obviously plays a significant role in protecting our Nation's companies and consumers. My written testimony spends a lot of time discussing that.

I would say two things we really focused on in the testimony was the necessity to get rid of static numbers in the environment. I think one of the things the President's Cyber Security Summit demonstrated was there was a lot of energy around having customers have to essentially remember things in digits and symbols to socially prove they are who they are, ways through biometrics and ways through tokenization and other ways to authenticate transactions.

Individuals are essentially going to be the mechanization by which I think we really can make a much greater impact on the fraud we are seeing today in the payments base and otherwise.

I do think from a technology standpoint, the other promising thing is STIX and TAXI which has also been discussed whereby we are developing a mechanism for even the smallest financial institution and the smallest health company to be able to consume data and spend more time analyzing that data as opposed to having to make a determination as to whether or not the data even has any meaning in their environment.

Those are my oral remarks. I look forward to your questions.

[Prepared Statement of Mr. Johnson follows:]

Testimony of
Wm. Douglas Johnson
On behalf of the
American Bankers Association
before the
Subcommittee on Information Technology
of the
Committee on Oversight and Government Reform
United States Senate

Thursday, March 5, 2015

Chairman Hurd, Ranking Member Kelly, members of the subcommittee, my name is Doug Johnson, Senior Vice President, Payments and Cybersecurity Policy, of the American Bankers Association (ABA). In that capacity, I currently lead the association's physical and cybersecurity, business continuity and resiliency policy and fraud deterrence efforts on behalf of our membership.

I appreciate the opportunity to be here to represent the ABA and discuss the importance of instituting a uniform federal data breach law in place of disparate state laws. The ABA is the voice of the nation's $15 trillion banking industry, which is composed of small, regional and large banks that together employ more than 2 million people, safeguard $11 trillion in deposits and extend over $8 trillion in loans.

I also currently serve as Vice Chairman of the Financial Services Sector Coordinating Council for Critical Infrastructure Protection and Homeland Security (FSSCC) and on the Board of Directors of the Financial Services Information Sharing and Analysis Center (FS-ISAC).

Established in 2002, the FSSCC is the national critical infrastructure protection coordinator for the financial sector, focused on operational risks. Because the FSSCC fits into a larger network of sector coordinating councils, it is uniquely positioned as the leader within financial services for developing strategies to improve shared critical infrastructure and homeland security.

Established in 1999, the FS-ISAC is the designated operational arm of the FSSCC. The Center supports the protection of the global financial services sector by assisting FSSCC, Treasury as well as regional agencies and entities to identify, prioritize and coordinate the protection of critical financial services, infrastructure service and key resources. The FS-ISAC also facilitates sharing of information pertaining to physical and cyber threats, vulnerabilities, incidents, potential protective measures and practices.

As the 114th Congress engages in public debate on the important issue of cybersecurity, we share your concerns regarding the evolving nature of cyber threats facing the private sector. The ABA, now through its Center for Payments and Cybersecurity Policy, has historically been very supportive of these collaborative efforts to protect our sector's and nation's cybersecurity. The financial sector is an acknowledged leader in defending against cyber threats. These efforts, in their sixteenth year, are highly mature and increasingly focused on international and cross-sectorial efforts to enhance our collective ability to defend against and respond to cybersecurity attacks. We support effective cyber security policy and will continue to work with Congress to achieve that goal.

In my testimony I will focus on three main points:

> **The evolving nature of cyber threats.**

> **The role of technology in addressing cyber threats.**

> **The role of expanded information sharing in protecting against these threats.**

I. The Evolving Nature of Cyber Threats

According to the recently released "Worldwide Threat Assessment of the US Intelligence Community," while cyber threats to US national and economic security are increasing in frequency, scale, sophistication, and severity of impact, and the range of cyber threat actors, methods of attack, targeted systems, and victims are also expanding,[the likelihood of a catastrophic attack from any particular actor is remote at this time]. This highlights the persistent and ever-changing nature of the threats the private sector faces and will face in the future.[1]

Attacks that once were singular in focus, be it a denial of service attack on financial institutions, an attack against merchant point-of-sale devices, or an attempt to destroy or wipe data of an energy company, may now contain a variety of such attack vectors. Such multi-faceted attacks create particular challenges for the victimized company or companies, necessitating the simultaneous maintenance of availability, integrity, and confidentiality of data when formerly a cyber-attack might have impact on only one of these vital data security components.

Attackers of every variety are also becoming increasingly adept at defeating security practices, increasing the velocity with which companies must move to ensure they understand how cyber risks are changing and what mitigating measures are most effective against these risks. It is indeed an arms race.

Another increasing challenge for financial institutions and the private sector generally is the need to digest an increasingly larger volume of cyber threat data. Determining the relevance of a particular piece of threat data, analyzing the magnitude of the threat, evaluating which systems might be impacted, and devising the appropriate course to take to mitigate the threat if necessary has become increasingly difficult.

Lastly, the victim of the attack is also changing. Prior to 2014, much of the private and public sector cyber security focus was on critical infrastructure and the payments system. Now there is recognition that, given the broader motivations of attackers for conducting a cyber-attack, essentially any company and any sector could be subject to a significant, highly visible attack.

---

[1] Statement for the Record, Worldwide Threat Assessment of the US Intelligence Community, Senate Armed Services Committee, James R. Clapper, Director of National Intelligence, February 26, 2015, available at: http://www.dni.gov/files/documents/Unclassified_2015_ATA_SFR_-_SASC_FINAL.pdf.

II. The Role of Technology in Addressing Cyber Threats

Technology obviously has a significant role in protecting our nation's companies and consumers from cyber threats. I would like to focus on two areas pertinent to today's hearing: technology used within our payment system and within our cyber threat information sharing environment.

The fact that attackers are becoming increasingly adept at defeating cybersecurity practices and mitigating measures points to the need for industry to develop and deploy enhanced measures on an ongoing basis with greater speed.

From the payment card technology standpoint, there is currently much discussion of the current roll-out of chip, or EMV payment card technology both at the point-of-sale and on the card itself. EMV technology consists of a small microprocessor chip embedded in a payment card, that an EMV-enabled point-of-sale device at a merchant can read, that encrypts card information. Utilizing EMV technology makes breached card data virtually useless to criminals wanting to replicate a card and use it physically at a merchant location. EMV technology does not, however, protect the card from being used online for purchases. A static card number, when compromised, could still be used for an unauthorized online purchase even if a chip was on the card.

Eliminating the use of static numbers altogether for debit and credit card purchases is a very important next step in protecting our payment system and the consumers that use it. Finding ways to keep consumers from having to remember static numbers, letters or symbols in order to authenticate themselves when conducting a financial or other sensitive transaction was a primary focus at the recent White House Summit on Cybersecurity and Consumer Protection. For instance:

> ➢ **Ajay Banga, President and CEO, MasterCard:** "What I have learned from my consumer customers is that they want two clear things aside from safety and security – one is to stop making me remember things to prove I am who I am. Because there are too many things to remember."[2]

---

[2] Ajay Banga, President and CEO, MasterCard, Remarks at The White House Summit Cybersecurity and Consumer Protection, Stanford University, February 13, 2015, available at: http://youtu.be/flcThSpCL.

> **Richard Davis, Chairman and CEO, US Bank:** "Our job is really a lot of financial literacy to help people understand how to protect themselves better...not putting a piece of tape on the back of your debit card or credit card and writing your PIN on it."[3]

> **Chuck Scharf, CEO, Visa:** We can talk all we want about methods of authentication...but the fact is if card numbers are flying around even though there is zero liability it's not something the consumer wants to go through...We are working with people across the payment ecosystem to figure out where we can get rid of those account numbers, so if there is a compromise, which there always will be because the bad guys are steps ahead as hard as we all try, the compromise does not have the effect it has today."[4]

These comments point to the fact that payment security is a dynamic challenge that requires a like response, and that there is no single solution that will eliminate payment fraud. Locking in *any* static technology provides a roadmap to attackers, telling them where to focus their attacks. While payment networks, financial institutions, and merchants are all working toward installing chip technology prior to the October 2015 deadline, we are already seeing a migration of fraud to online, card not present transactions that chip technology cannot address, but tokenization can. Tokenization replaces sensitive consumer account information at the register or online with a random "token," rendering any static information associated with the transaction useless to criminals, and thus shows great promise.

Another technological area that shows great promise is the FS-ISAC effort to automate the analysis and distribution of cyber threat data to the greatest extent possible. As I have already noted, the significant amount of threat information now being received by financial institutions has created increased difficulty in determining the relevance of a particular piece of threat data. There is a real danger, as our sector expands our information sharing capabilities to an increasing number of smaller financial institutions and outside the financial sector, that the sheer volume of threat information creates an unintended barrier to effective participation in threat information sharing.

---

[3] Richard Davis, Chairman and CEO, US Bank, Remarks at The White House Summit Cybersecurity and Consumer Protection, Stanford University, February 13, 2015, available at: http://youtu.be/KNnyfio2o-pc.
[4] Chuck Scharf, CEO, Visa, Remarks at The White House Summit Cybersecurity and Consumer Protection, Stanford University, February 13, 2015, available at: http://youtu.be/jo_I6V-H8Xs.

To counteract this possibility, the FS-ISAC in concert with the Depository Trust and Clearing Corporation established Soltra, a strategic joint venture formed to utilize two new standards, Structured Threat Information eXpression (STIX) and Trusted Automated eXchange of Indicator Information (TAXI) to develop an automated mechanism to receive and send cyber threat information machine to machine and dramatically reduce the effort and workload associated with threat intelligence.

The mechanism, called Soltra Edge, is able to automatically read and categorize threat indicators through STIX and then transmit them computer to computer via TAXI. While the Soltra Edge is currently used predominately by larger financial institutions, the system has recently been made available to smaller financial institutions free of charge. We also expect this solution to be adopted broadly by many critical sectors such as healthcare, energy, transportation, and retail.

The deployment of STIX and TAXI through the FS-ISAC is an excellent example of a set of standards initially developed by MITRE and the Department of Homeland Security (DHS) that now have an important commercial application that will greatly benefit the overall cybersecurity posture of our nation.

III. The Role of Expanded Information Sharing in Protecting against Cyber Threats

Recent cyber-attacks underscore the need to help *all* businesses improve their awareness of threats and enhance their response capabilities. The steps taken by the Administration, through the issuance of the February 13, 2015, executive order promoting private sector cybersecurity information sharing, will help the business community and government agencies share critical threat information more effectively.

While the recent executive order is an important step towards more effective information sharing, it is widely recognized that Congress must also act to pass legislation to fill important gaps that executive action cannot fill. For instance, legislation is necessary to give businesses legal certainty that they have safe harbor against frivolous lawsuits when voluntarily sharing and receiving threat indicators and countermeasures in real time and taking actions to mitigate cyberattacks. Legislation also needs to offer protections related to public disclosure, regulatory, and antitrust matters in order to increase the timely exchange of information among public and private entities. ABA also believes that legislation needs to safeguard privacy and civil liberties and establish appropriate roles for civilian and intelligence agencies. The financial sector is dedicated to protecting customer data, and has led the way for effective information sharing through the development of the FS-ISAC. We are committed to working with others within the overall business community to develop a similarly strong and effective mechanism for sharing threat information.

I will focus on two important areas within the executive order: the acceleration of the DHS security clearance process and the establishment of Information Sharing and Analysis Organizations (ISAOs).

Information sharing is of critical importance to the financial services sector, other critical infrastructure sectors and the government. Without it, none of the financial sector's security and resiliency priorities would be achievable. With key federal support from the Treasury Department as our Sector Specific Agency, law enforcement and DHS, our network defenders are better able to prepare for cyber threats when there is a consistent, reliable and sustainable flow of actionable cybersecurity information and analysis, at both a classified and unclassified level.

As a nation, we are making some progress toward this goal, but it has become increasingly necessary for appropriately-cleared representatives of critical sectors such as financial services to have access, and provide contributions, to classified information that enables analysts and operators to take timely action to defend essential systems. Accordingly, the executive order's enhancement of DHS's role in accelerating the security clearance process for critical sector owners and operators is a clear indication of the Administration's support for this public-private partnership.

The ISAC's have played an important role for critical infrastructure protection information sharing and incident response for their sectors. The FS-ISAC, in particular, enjoys strong support from sector members, Treasury and DHS. In this spirit, we also support the creation of ISAOs as a mechanism for all sectors, regions and other stakeholder groups to share cybersecurity information and coordinate analysis and response. While ISACs must retain their status as the government's primary critical infrastructure partners, given their mandate for broad sectoral representation, the development of ISAOs should be facilitated for stakeholder groups that require a collaborative cyber and physical threat information sharing capability that builds on the strong foundation laid by the ISACs.

As the ISAO standards development process unfolds, certain principles must be upheld for structuring both the ISAOs themselves and the government's interaction with them:

➤ Sharing of sensitive security information within and among communities of trust is successful when operational standards of practice establish clear and enforced information handling rules;

➤ Information sharing is not a competitive sport: while competition in innovation can improve technical capabilities, operational standards should incentivize federated information sharing. Threat and vulnerability intelligence needs to be fused across trust communities, not diffused or siloed;

➤ Government internal processes for collecting, analyzing and packaging critical infrastructure protection intelligence for ISAC/ISAO consumption must be streamlined and transparent to maximize timeliness, accuracy and relevance of actionable shared information; and

➤ To manage scarce resources, government information sharing mechanisms such as the National Cyber and Communications Integration Center (NCCIC) and the Treasury Department's Cyber Intelligence Group (CIG) should prioritize engagements with ISACs and ISAOs according to transparently established criteria.

It is also important that the process to develop the ISAO standards is collaborative, open, and transparent. The process managed by the National Institute of Standards and Technology (NIST) during the development of the NIST Cybersecurity Framework is an excellent example of the appropriate leveraging of private sector input, knowledge and experience to develop guidance that will primarily impact non-governmental entities. We encourage DHS, as the implementing authority of the president's EO, to emulate the engagement model that NIST used to create and adopt their Cybersecurity Framework. The process worked.

Finally, for DHS to be successful implementing the EO and its many cyber security risk management and partnership authorities, it must be sufficiently resourced with the best analytical and technical capabilities, with a cadre of highly qualified cybersecurity leaders and analytical teams to conduct its mission. There must be a concerted effort to recruit, retain and maintain a world class workforce that is able to assess cyber threats globally and help the private sector reduce risk to this nation. With the application of the principles discussed in this statement, we believe the creation of ISAOs and their partnership agreements with DHS have the potential to complement the ISAC foundation and measurably improve cyber risk reduction for critical infrastructure and the national economy.

IV. The Path Forward

We look forward to working with Congress, the Administration and DHS to leverage the FS-ISAC as a successful model in the development of regional information sharing and analysis organizations. Above all, we urge Congress to send a bill to the president that gives businesses the liability and antitrust protections, and our citizens the privacy and civil liberty protections that will enhance our already significant efforts to protect the cybersecurity of our nation.

Mr. HURD. Thank you, Mr. Johnson.
Mr. Mierzwinski, please.

STATEMENT OF EDMUND MIERZWINSKI

Mr. MIERZWINSKI. Thank you, Mr. Chairman, Representative Kelly and members of the committee.

I am Ed Mierzwinski of the U.S. Public Interest Research Group.

In my oral remarks, I want to talk about some of the threats that consumers face from the large amount of their information that is floating around in cyber space and is often obtained by hackers and other people intent on doing evil.

I identify in my written testimony, three levels of breach. The first level is a simple card number breach. A card number breach results in what is called existing account fraud. It is a problem but consumers are generally well protected by law in the case of existing account fraud.

If, of course, your debit card is breached, you do have the additional problem of losing money from your bank account until the bank puts the money back in. That is why consumer advocates recommend the use of credit cards, if you can avoid credit card debt.

The second level of breach is a breach that also obtains email names, email addresses, telephone numbers, the sort of information that allows the bad guy to conduct what is called phishing expeditions to try to obtain additional information about you.

I should point out that after any big breach, it is not only the serious bad guy that got into your account that conducts phishing expeditions, it is anybody with an email list can then send mail out to people and say, hey, if you are a person who shopped at Target, we need your information.

They are not even the guy that has part of your information. They are just another bad guy hoping to capitalize on it. It is a serious problem.

The third level of breach is the one that results in the mother lode of information being collected that allows worse harm to directly be conducted against you. Phishing expeditions are designed to collect your Social Security number but the Anthem breach and now the Premera breach resulted in the breach of Social Security numbers which can be used to easily to commit financial identity theft which is a problem that has been around for 20 years.

The additional problem of tax refund identity theft has been around fewer years but is something worthy of the committee's further review and another hearing probably.

Third is medical identity theft where bad guys get medical attention in your name because they take advantage of your good medical insurance to get their own medical treatment.

The fourth kind of problem many consumers have faced over the years—I have talked to Secret Service agents about this—is a bad guy with the bad name wants to use your name to commit crime because you might not be in the system, you do not have two strikes against you already.

There are also emotional and other problems that people face from identity theft.

What can consumers do? Often companies recommend credit monitoring. In the Anthem and Premera breaches, I say take the credit monitoring. In an existing account breach, it does not help. It will not stop identity theft. It is a sop, something that will cause you to think you are better protected than you actually are.

We recommend any consumer who is not directly in the market for new credit to get a security freeze. My testimony goes into detail on how the security freeze is really the only way to protect your credit report.

We recommend to Congress, as committees of jurisdiction can consider legislation, do not preempt the States. The States are privacy leaders. Do not impose any sort of harm trigger in any breach legislation. Use an acquisition trigger.

If a company loses your information, it should not have the right to decide whether to tell you. It should have its own reputation at risk. Use a broad definition of personally identifiable information in any legislation that goes forward.

Most of the bills that I have seen are narrower than State laws. The Attorney General of Illinois has just proposed amendments to their State law, for example, that add geo-locational and marketing information to the definition of personal information.

Information is no longer just tracked in computers but tracked on your smart phone. Geo-location is very important.

As Mr. French talked about, we totally agree with the merchant's technology neutral performance standard. Chip and pin is the highest current standard. Why are the banks stopping at chip and signature? It is illogical.

Apple Pay and tokenization have some hope but Apple Pay has been breached in low tech ways, so a lot more needs to be done there.

My testimony concludes by going into some detail on the general ecosystem we have today that simply collects too much information and keeps it for too long. Consumers need privacy rights based on a robust of code fair information practices.

Thank you for the opportunity to testify.

[Prepared Statement of Mr. Mierzwinski follows:]

Testimony of Edmund Mierzwinski

U.S. PIRG Consumer Program Director

at a hearing on

"Cybersecurity: The Evolving Nature of Cyber Threats Facing the Private Sector"

Before the House Committee on Oversight and Government Reform

Subcommittee on Information Technology

Honorable William Hurd, Chair

18 March 2015

**Testimony of Edmund Mierzwinski, U.S. PIRG Consumer Program Director at a hearing
on "Cybersecurity: The Evolving Nature of Cyber Threats Facing the Private Sector"
House Subcommittee on Information Technology, 18 March 2015**

Chairman Hurd, Representative Kelly, members of the committee, I appreciate the opportunity to testify before you on the important matter of cyber threats, which I construe broadly in this testimony to include not only data breaches but also generally accepted industry practices that may actually be unfair to consumers. Since 1989, I have worked on data privacy issues, among other financial system and consumer protection issues, for the U.S. Public Interest Research Group. The state PIRGs are non-profit, non-partisan public interest advocacy organizations that take on powerful interests on behalf of their members.

Summary:

The authoritative Privacy Rights Clearinghouse has estimated that since 2005, at least 815,842,526 records have been breached in a total of at least 4,495 data breach occurrences made public since 2005.[1] One of the latest exploits, against Anthem, a health insurance company, not only affected up to 80 million consumers, but compromised among the richest troves of personal information I have seen in my 25 years of privacy research.

Data collectors collect and save too much information on consumers, keep it too long and often use it without consumer knowledge, let alone permission. While consumer and privacy organizations believe we need a robust Consumer Privacy Bill of Rights, based on a strong version of the Code of Fair Information Practices, in the short run we need to address the failure of data collectors – including retailers, banks, universities, government agencies, health insurers and others – to protect customer information from misuse. Data breaches, hacks and misuse cost the economy billions of dollars and cause profound harms to consumers.

It is important that policymakers understand that you cannot bifurcate the issues of data security and privacy. Consumer privacy is threatened when data collectors do not keep data secure. In the new Big Data world, where firms are racing to vacuum up even more data than ever before, with even less acknowledgement of any privacy interest by consumers (or citizens), it is important that we re-establish norms that give consumers and citizens greater control over the collection, and use, of their personal information.

In the immediate circumstance, the best way to give consumers protection against data breaches is to hold firms that lose their information accountable. Threats to consumers can include fraud on existing accounts, new account identity theft, medical identity theft, tax refund identity theft and imposters committing crimes using your identity. Measurable harms from these misuses are obvious, but any measure of harms must also include the cost and time spent cleaning these problems up, additional problems caused by an empty checking account or a missing tax refund

---

[1] See "Chronology of Data Breaches." Privacy Rights Clearinghouse, last visited 15 March 2015, https://www.privacyrights.org/data-breach.

and being denied or paying more for credit or insurance or rejected for jobs due to the digital carnage caused by the thief. Consumers also face very real emotional stress and even trauma from financial distress.

Cyber security problems are caused by a variety of factors. Banks blame merchants for shoddy card security. While banks expect merchants to build higher cyber walls every year, only recently have they begrudgingly begun to take steps to phase out their obsolete, reckless 40-year old magnetic stripe credit and debit card technologies. Even now, however, the banks would prefer to move only incrementally, to Chip and Signature cards, even though a more secure technology, Chip and PIN, has been around for years in other countries. The Chip ensures that your card is not a clone; the PIN ensures that you are not an imposter. Nevertheless, policymakers should embrace neither technology, but should take steps to urge firms to use the best-available technology-neutral technologies. Of course, these card changes only will reduce retail point-of-sale fraud; the threat of card-not-present fraud (such as Internet purchases) requires additional improvements.

In my testimony, I will discuss these and other issues that our failure to enforce adequate data security has on consumers. I rely on the other witnesses today to explain the problems banks, merchants and other firms face. On some matters, we may even agree. I caution the Congress, however, not to move forward on any breach or data security legislation that would preempt strong state privacy leadership or would endorse closed or non-technology neutral standards. Federal law should never become a ceiling of protection, it should always serve as a minimal floor that allows state experimentation. Further, federal law should not endorse specific solutions that limit innovation.

I. Some Breaches Involve Card Numbers, Others Are Worse

It is important to understand that not all breaches are created equal. Here is a rough hierarchy, in ascending order of harm to consumers.

1) Card Number Breach: When merchant terminals are breached, typically the only information stolen is credit and debit card numbers. These numbers can only be used for what is called existing account fraud. While this costs the banks or merchants money, consumers are generally well-protected by law from bearing the costs of any frauds. Credit card fraud liability is limited by law to $50; debit card liability is zero if the consumer notifies the institution within 60 days (when only the number, but not the device) is stolen.[2] In the case of debit cards, of course, the consumer may face the additional problem of bouncing other checks until the bank returns her money to her account. That is why every consumer advocate I know recommends that consumers who can avoid the temptation of carrying credit card debt only use credit cards at

---

[2] Debit card liability is much higher if the card is stolen, and liability increases dramatically after 60 days. http://www.uspirgedfund.org/news/usp/groups-offer-consumer-tips-after-target-data-breach (last visited 3 March 2015).

retail or online. Unfortunately, however, only a very small number of banks and credit unions offer PIN-only ATM cards; nearly all only offer "debit cards" that can be used at ATMs with a PIN but also at point of sale with just a swipe and signature.

2) Phishing, When General Customer Information (email/phone/address) also Breached: Obtaining a consumer's email address allows the thief to make "phishing" attacks, hoping the consumer will click a link that allows a virus to invade her computer and obtain more information – such as bank account passwords, or Social Security Numbers, etc. Obtaining a phone number associated with a known bank or other account allows the thief to make "social engineering" phone calls, hoping to use the small amount of information that they have to trick the consumer into giving up more. Spear-phishing is a more sophisticated variant where the thief is looking for targeted information from employees of certain companies or agencies, for the secondary purpose of industrial, or state-sponsored, espionage.

The additional information the bad guys seek, then, would either allow them direct access to your existing account (through the PIN or credit card security code (CVV) that they didn't have before) or to open new accounts in your name (with your Social Security Number) by committing identity theft. They use what they know to convince you to tell them what they don't know. They want your PIN, or your birthdate or Social Security Number. They hope to trick you into giving it up.

3) Social Security Numbers and other Details Breached: The Social Security Number is the key that unlocks your credit report and tax refund. Armed with a social security number, a thief can apply for new accounts in your name. The thief doesn't breach your report. He provides a creditor with an application containing your Social Security Number but his address. Such financial identity theft lowers your credit score, causing you to be denied credit or jobs. Cleaning up financial identity theft can be a nightmare for consumers, despite a number of changes that were made to the Fair Credit Reporting Act in 2003.

Worse, convincing the IRS that a thief obtained your tax refund before you were able to file is similarly a nightmare for consumers that takes 3-6 months or more to clean up (and only then obtain your refund). While Intuit Turbotax continues to deny that it was breached in a recent incident involving thousands of state returns, not only do security experts[3] contend that the firm failed to use best practices to verify taxpayer identities but state tax officials[4] also argue that it failed to respond to their warnings. As the Washington Post explained:

---

[3] Brian Krebs argues that Intuit not only did not use email and phone validation, it did not confirm account changes with customers or use "Know-Your-Customer" validation (until after the breach), "Intuit Failed at 'Know Your Customer' Basics," 15 March 2015, Krebs On Security, http://krebsonsecurity.com/2015/03/intuit-failed-at-know-your-customer-basics/ (last visited 15 March 2015).

[4] Julie P. Magee, Alabama Commissioner of Revenue, "It's Time to Adopt a Common Objective to Stop Fraudulent Tax Refunds," 12 March 2015, https://www.linkedin.com/pulse/its-time-adopt-common-objective-stop-fraudulent-tax-julie (last visited 15 March 2015).

"The hackers who targeted TurboTax this year appeared to use two techniques. Some seemed to already have people's personal information and created fake accounts to submit phony tax returns. Others figured out users' log-ins and passwords, by trying multiple iterations, and gained wide access to their accounts."[5]

II. Why the Anthem Breach Was So Bad

The Target retail breach affected two overlapping groups of customers. Some had their credit or debit card numbers "RAM-scraped" from the retail terminal system before the information even entered the encryption module of the firm's computers. But the thieves also rooted around inside Target's computers and obtained additional general customer information, including email addresses and phone numbers, for consumers with registered Target accounts. The first set of consumers would be at risk of existing account fraud; the second set would be vulnerable to phishing expeditions. Phishing is a threat, but contrast that with Anthem.

According to widespread news reports,[6] the Anthem breach struck a mother lode of consumer data. The theft included information on up to 80 million consumers (including some non-Anthem customers in related plans) and the data points taken included the names of employers, birth dates, social security numbers, medical account numbers, phone numbers, and home and email addresses (but no medical records). Experts believe that the Anthem data will hold strong value to thieves for years (while card numbers decline rapidly in black market value).

These data points could be used to commit a variety of more serious frauds, including obtaining your tax refund, obtaining medical care in your name and also committing financial identity theft, when new accounts are opened in your name by the thief. Names of employers and work emails could be used for spear-phishing attacks on those firms' servers. Anthem has sent its customers a general e-mail notice and posted a website, anthemfacts.com, indicating it is conducting additional "forensics," and will notify customers by regular mail if they were actually breached, upon its completion.

1) Many people have not even heard of medical ID theft. As the World Privacy Forum explains:

> "Medical identity theft occurs when someone uses a person's name and sometimes other parts of their identity — such as insurance information — without the person's knowledge or consent to obtain medical services or goods, or uses the person's identity information to make false claims for medical services or goods. Medical identity theft frequently results in erroneous entries being put into existing medical records, and can involve the creation of fictitious medical records in the victim's name. Medical identity theft is a crime that can cause great harm to its victims. Yet

---

[5] Jonnelle Marte and Craig Timberg, "Who's to blame when fraudsters use TurboTax to steal refunds?" 4 March 2015, The Washington Post, http://www.washingtonpost.com/news/get-there/wp/2015/03/04/unprecedented-surge-in-online-tax-scams-raises-questions-about-turbotax/ (last visited 15 March 2015).
[6] Chad Terhune, "U.S., states probe massive data breach at health insurer Anthem," 6 Feb 2015, Los Angeles Times, http://www.latimes.com/business/la-fi-anthem-hack-20150207-story.html (last visited 3 March 2015)

despite the profound risk it carries, it is the least studied and most poorly documented of the cluster of identity theft crimes. It is also the most difficult to fix after the fact, because victims have limited rights and recourses. Medical identity theft typically leaves a trail of falsified information in medical records that can plague victims' medical and financial lives for years."[7]

2) What Can Potential Anthem Breach Victims Do? Anthem is providing a free credit monitoring service to its customers. While we and other consumer groups do not recommend taking credit monitoring if you are a victim solely of a card number breach that could result in existing account fraud, because it doesn't do any good in that circumstance and promotes a false sense of hope, we have no real objection to accepting it in this instance. Certainly, however, never pay for it.[8] We recommend that consumers who even suspect they are identity theft victims add a 90-day, renewable initial fraud alert to their credit reports (which also entitles you to an additional free credit report).[9] Watch your health and medical records statements carefully for at least two years to avoid medical identity theft. Take advantage of additional tips from World Privacy Forum.[10]

3) Next, Place a Security Freeze: Better yet, we encourage victims of the Anthem breach to place a security freeze on each of their credit reports. Indeed, any consumer who wants to proactively prevent misuse of her credit should consider a freeze. Over ten years ago U.S. PIRG, along with Consumers Union, drafted a model state security freeze law, and with the help of AARP and others, it rapidly became law in 47 states. At that point, even the generally recalcitrant credit bureaus finally capitulated and agreed to provide freezes in all jurisdictions. A security freeze prevents "new" credit from being issued in your name but allows your existing creditors to look at your report. It is the only way to prevent financial identity theft, since new creditors who cannot see credit scores or reports will not open new accounts. A freeze requires more work by you; if you want to apply for a car loan, new credit card or a home re-fi, you'll need to temporarily "lift" the freeze (you can do this on a selective or general creditor basis). A typical freeze costs $10 ($30 for 3) and $5-10 each time it is temporarily lifted. A few states

---

[7] World Privacy Forum, "Medical Identity Theft" page, http://www.worldprivacyforum.org/category/med-id-theft/ (last visited 15 March 1015). The page also lists a blog dated 6 Feb 2015, "Medical ID Theft a Threat for Anthem Breach Victims, Key Tips" http://www.worldprivacyforum.org/2015/02/medical-id-theft-a-threat-for-anthem-breach-victims-key-tips/ (last visited 15 March 2015).

[8] However, credit monitoring firms often insist, in their terms of service, that a consumer agree that any issues be resolved through pre-dispute, or forced, arbitration. We support action by the Consumer Financial Protection Bureau or legislation to ban pre-dispute arbitration in any consumer contract, but it is especially onerous when the consumer needs the service offered because some company allowed her information to be stolen. Any federal breach legislation should ban arbitration clauses in any services offered by a breached entity or its vendors.

[9] If you know you are an identity theft victim and file a police report or FTC affidavit demonstrating this, you can request a permanent fraud alert. More at http://www.consumer.ftc.gov/features/feature-0014-identity-theft (last visited 2 March 2015).

[10] World Privacy Forum, "Medical ID Theft a Threat for Anthem Breach Victims, Key Tips," 6 February 2015, http://www.worldprivacyforum.org/2015/02/medical-id-theft-a-threat-for-anthem-breach-victims-key-tips/ (last visited 15 March 2015).

offer free security freezes for identity theft victims or senior citizens.[11] Free security freezes for all consumers would be a logical enhancement for policymakers to consider to the federal, or state, Fair Credit Reporting Acts. While freezes are not yet free, they are much less expensive than paid credit monitoring and infinitely more effective.

III. What Steps Should Congress Take?

Congress should move carefully on data security. There is potential to benefit consumers but there is potential to make things worse.

1) Don't Override the States with A Weak Data Breach Notification Law, Especially with Broad Data Security Law Preemption: Congress should carefully weigh its response to the increase in breaches. We believe that federal breach notification legislation is unnecessary (because all firms need to do is comply with the strongest state law) and that such legislation, if it were to preempt stronger state action on data security or privacy protection, would be unwise. Most of the breach bills I have reviewed are weaker than state laws and include Trojan Horse preemption provisions eliminating not only state breach laws, but all future state actions to protect data security or privacy. That's the wrong response. Many federal proposals are also weak because they contain a "harm trigger" that allows the firm that lost your information to decide whether to tell you. Decision-making for whether to require breach notification should not be placed in the hands of a sloppy breached entity.

2) Consider Upgrades to Card Protections: Increasing consumer protections under the Electronic Funds Transfer Act (EFTA), which applies to debit cards, to the gold standard levels of the Truth in Lending Act, which applies to credit cards, should be considered. In some circumstances, consumers who lose a debit card are liable for all the money in their accounts (although they are generally well-protected if only the card data, but not the device, are taken.) Facing higher liability may "focus the mind" of the banks on improving security. Further, with new card (pre-paid cards) and device (smart phone and other technologies) being developed, it makes sense to ensure that all consumer payment systems are equally protected.

3) Rein in Credit Monitoring Advertising: Congress should also investigate the deceptive marketing of subscription-based credit monitoring, ID theft insurance, debt cancellation and other add-on products, which are over-priced and often provide a false sense of security. Credit monitoring services won't stop or warn of fraud on existing accounts. The product from Experian that was provided by Target (protectmyid) won't stop identity theft, it will simply notify you after the fact of changes to your Experian credit report (but not to your Trans Union or Equifax reports, which may include different account information). Positively, that offered product terminated after one year, rather than auto-renewing for a monthly fee (when similar products were offered after some previous breaches, the over-priced, under-performing credit

---

[11] Learn more about security freezes from Consumers Union here.
http://consumersunion.org/research/consumers-unions-guide-to-security-freeze-protection/

monitoring products were sometimes set to auto-renew for a fee). The products unwisely provide consumers at risk of existing account fraud a false sense of security.[12]

4) Don't Place All Blame on Merchants for Payment Card Breaches: Despite my reservations about Target's and other breached merchants') delayed and drawn out notifications to customers about their breaches and their provision of often inadequate credit monitoring product, I don't believe that Target or other merchants deserve all of the blame for the data breaches that occur on their watch.

5) The card networks are also largely at fault. They have continued to use an obsolete 1970s magnetic stripe technology well into the 21st century. When the technology was solely tied to credit cards, where consumers enjoy strong fraud rights and other consumer protections by law, this may have been barely tolerable. But when the big banks and credit card networks asked consumers to expose their own bank accounts to the unsafe signature-based payment system, by piggybacking once safer PIN-only debit cards onto the signature-based system, the omission became unacceptable. The vaunted "zero-liability" promises of the card networks and issuing banks are by contract, not law. Of course, the additional problem any debit card fraud victim faces is that she is missing money from her own account while the bank conducts an allowable reinvestigation for ten days or more, even if the bank eventually lives up to its promise.[13]

Further, the card networks' failure to upgrade, let alone enforce, their PCI or security standards, despite the massive revenue stream provided by consumers and merchants through swipe, or interchange, fees, is yet another problem caused, not by the merchants, but by the banks and card networks.

Further, the Federal Reserve Board's rule interpreting the Durbin amendment limiting swipe fees on the debit cards of the biggest banks also provides for additional fraud revenue to the banks in several ways. Even though banks and card networks routinely pass along virtually all costs of fraud to merchants in the form of chargebacks, the Fed rule interpreting the Durbin amendment allows for much more revenue. In many ways, the merchants are as much victims of the banks' unsecure systems as consumers are.[14]

---

[12] Even worse, consumers who accept the monitoring product, protectmyid from the credit bureau Experian, must accept a boilerplate forced arbitration clause that restricts their ability to sue Experian. See http://www.protectmyid.com/terms/ And under current U.S. Supreme Court jurisprudence, that clause's outrageous ban on joining a class action is also permissible.

[13] Compare some of the Truth In Lending Act's robust credit card protections by law to the Electronic Funds Transfer Act's weak debit card consumer rights at this FDIC website: http://www.fdic.gov/consumers/consumer/news/cnfall09/debit_vs_credit.html

[14] In October 2015, changes to the PCI liability system take effect that require either the merchant or the creditor, whichever one has not upgraded, to have greater contractual liability. See, for example, http://www.businesswire.com/news/home/20150212005260/en/U.S.-POS-Terminals-EMV-Chip-Enabled-Year-End-2015# (last visited 15 March 2015).

IV. Detailed Recommendations:

1) Congress should not enact any federal breach law that preempts state breach laws or, especially, includes Trojan Horse preemption of other state data security rights: We make this point above. But here is more detail. In 2003, when Congress, in the FACT Act, amended the Fair Credit Reporting Act, it specifically did not preempt the right of the states to enact stronger data security and identity theft protections. We argued that since Congress hadn't solved all the problems, it shouldn't prevent the states from doing so.

From 2004-today, 46 states enacted security breach notification laws and 49 states or territories enacted security freeze laws. Many of these laws were based on the CLEAN Credit and Identity Theft Protection Model State Law developed by Consumers Union and U.S. PIRG.

A security freeze, not credit monitoring, is the best way to prevent identity theft. If a consumer places a security freeze on her credit reports, a criminal can apply for credit in her name, but the new potential creditor cannot access your "frozen" credit report and will reject the application. The freeze is not for everyone, since you must unfreeze your report on a specific or general basis whenever you re-enter the credit marketplace, but it is only way to protect your credit report from unauthorized access. See this Consumers Union page for a list of security freeze rights.

The other problem with enacting a preemptive federal breach notification law is that industry lobbyists will seek language that not only preempts breach notification laws but also prevents states from enacting any future data security laws, despite the laudable 2003 FACT Act example above. This is the Trojan Horse problem. A small federal gain should not result in a big rollback of state authority.

Simply as an example, S. 1927 (Carper) in the last Congress included sweeping preemption language that is unacceptable to consumer and privacy groups and likely also to most state attorneys general:

SEC. 7. RELATION TO STATE LAW. No requirement or prohibition may be imposed under the laws of any State with respect to the responsibilities of any person to—

(1) protect the security of information relating to consumers that is maintained or communicated by, or on behalf of, the person;

(2) safeguard information relating to consumers from potential misuse;

(3) investigate or provide notice of the unauthorized access to information relating to consumers, or the potential misuse of the information, for fraudulent, illegal, or other purposes; or

(4) mitigate any loss or harm resulting from the unauthorized access or misuse of information relating to consumers.

Other bills before the Congress have included similar, if not even more sweeping, abuses of our federal system. Such broad preemption will prevent states from acting as first responders to emerging privacy threats. Congress should not preempt the states but instead always enact a floor of protection. In fact, Congress should think twice about whether a federal breach law that is weaker than the best state laws is needed at all.

2) Congress should improve debit/ATM card consumer rights and provide consumers with strong fraud rights not matter what card or new device they use in the payment system: Up until now, both banks and merchants have looked at fraud and identity theft as a modest cost of doing business and have not protected the payment system well enough. They have failed to look seriously at harms to their customers from fraud and identity theft – including not just monetary losses and the hassles of restoring their good names, but also the emotional harm that they must face as they wonder whether future credit applications will be rejected due to the fraudulent accounts.

Currently, debit card fraud victims are reimbursed at "zero liability" only by promise. The EFTA's fraud standard actually provides for 3-tiers of consumer fraud losses. Consumers lose up to $50 if they notify the bank within two days of learning of the fraud, up to $500 if they notify the bank within 60 days and up to their entire loss, including from any linked accounts, if they notify the bank after 60 days. **However, if the physical debit card itself is not lost or stolen, consumers are not liable for any fraud charges if they report them within 60 days of their bank statement.**

This shared risk fraud standard under the EFTA, which governs debit cards, appears to be vestigial, or left over from the days when debit cards could only be used with a PIN. Since banks encourage consumers to use debit cards, placing their bank accounts at risk, on the unsafe signature debit platform, this fraud standard should be changed. Congress should also provide debit and prepaid card customers with the stronger billing dispute rights and rights to dispute payment for products that do not arrive or do not work as promised that credit card users enjoy (through the Fair Credit Billing Act, a part of the Truth In Lending Act).[15]

Debit/ATM card customers already face the aforementioned cash flow and bounced check problems while banks investigate fraud under the Electronic Funds Transfer Act. Reducing their possible liability by law, not simply by promise, won't solve this particular problem, but it will force banks to work harder to avoid fraud. If they face greater liability to their customers and accountholders, they will be more likely to develop better security. Further, this review by policymakers should also ensure that improvements in consumer protection extend to all new forms of payment, including prepaid cards, smart phones and emerging technologies.

---

[15] For a detailed discussion of these problems and recommended solutions, see Hillebrand, Gail (2008) "Before the Grand Rethinking: Five Things to Do Today with Payments Law and Ten Principles to Guide New Payments Products and New Payments Law," Chicago-Kent Law Review: Vol. 83, Iss. 2, Article 12, available at http://scholarship.kentlaw.iit.edu/cklawreview/vol83/iss2/12

3) Congress should not endorse a specific technology, such as EMV (parent technology of Chip and PIN and Chip and Signature). If Congress takes steps to encourage use of higher standards, its actions should be technology-neutral and apply equally to all players. Chip and PIN and Chip and signature are variants of the EMV technology standard commonly in use in Europe. The current slow U.S. rollout of Chip cards will generally provide less-secure Chip and Signature cards rather than the more-secure Chip and PIN cards. Why not go to the higher Chip and PIN authentication standard immediately and skip past Chip and Signature? Further, in his October executive order on payment card security, the President announced that all new government-issued cards would be Chip and PIN, not merely Chip and Signature.[16]

Of course, Congress should not embrace a specific technology. Instead, it should take steps to encourage all users to use the <u>highest possible, best available technology-neutral</u> performance standard. Congress should also take steps to ensure that additional technological improvements and security innovations are not blocked by actions or rules of the existing players or standards bodies.

If Congress does choose to impose higher standards, it must impose them equally on all players. For example, current legislative proposals may unwisely impose softer regimes on financial institutions already subject to the weaker Gramm-Leach-Bliley rules than to merchants and other non-financial institutions. Congress should also look at the weak requirements of the Health Insurance Portability and Accountability Act (HIPAA), which does not even require encryption.

Further, as most observers are aware, Chip technology will only prevent the use of cloned cards in card-present (Point-of-Sale) transactions. It is an improvement over obsolete magnetic stripe technology in that regard, yet it will have no impact on online transactions, where fraud volume is much greater already than in point-of-sale transactions. Experiments, such as with "virtual card numbers" for one-time use, are being carried out online. It would be worthwhile for the committee to inquire of the industry and the regulators how well those experiments are proceeding and whether requiring the use of virtual card numbers in all online debit and credit transactions should be considered a best practice.

Further, had Chip and PIN (or Chip and Signature) been in use, it would not have stopped most retail breaches, such as the Target breach, since card information was "RAM-scraped" from the Target system's internal RAM memory, after the cards had already been used but before data were encrypted.

Technologies such as Apple-Pay offer additional promise, but are often not as good as they are trumped up to be. Recently, "low-tech" thieves figured out that they could use forged or stolen or

---

[16] The White House, "Executive Order --Improving the Security of Consumer Financial Transactions," 17 October 2014, available at https://www.whitehouse.gov/the-press-office/2014/10/17/executive-order-improving-security-consumer-financial-transactions (last visited 16 March 2015).

cloned cards on the Apple Pay system because banks were not verifying that the card entered into the phone was itself legitimate.[17]

4) Investigate Card Security Standards Bodies and Ask the Prudential Regulators for Their Views: To ensure that improvements continue to be made in the system, the committee should also inquire into the governance and oversight of the development of card network security standards. Do regulators sit on the PCI board? As I understand it, merchants do not; they are only allowed to sit on what may be a meaningless "advisory" board. Further, do regulators have any mandatory oversight function over standards body rules? Are standards bodies open or closed? Does a closed standards body serve the public interest?

5) Congress should <u>not</u> enact any new legislation sought by some banks and credit unions to impose their costs of replacement cards on the merchants by law: Breached merchants should pay their share but breaches are not entirely a merchant's fault when the merchant has been forced to build an ever-higher wall to protect a dangerous, defective device, the magnetic stripe card. Disputes over costs of replacement cards should be handled by contracts and agreements between the players. How could you possibly draft a bill to address all the possible shared liabilities? Further, going forward, amendments to the PCI rules will impose greater liability on firms that have not adopted higher standards. For example, if a merchant's technology does not accept CHIP cards, it would face greater liability. If a merchant does accept CHIP cards, but the bank has not replaced its magnetic stripe cards, the bank would face higher liability.

6) Congress Should Allow Private Enforcement and Broad State and Local Enforcement of Any Law It Passes: The marketplace only works when we have strong federal laws and strong federal enforcement of those laws, buttressed by strong state and local and private enforcement.

Many of the data breach bills I have seen specifically state that no private right of action is created. Such clauses should be eliminated and it should also be made clear that the bills have no effect on any of the 17 state law private rights of action. Further, no bill should include language reducing the scope of state Attorney General <u>or</u> other state-level public official enforcement. Further, any federal law should not restrict state enforcement only to state Attorneys General, but allow enforcement by local enforcers, such as district attorneys.

7) No Federal Breach Law Should Include Any "Harm Trigger" Before Notice Is Required: The better state breach laws, including California and Illinois among others, require breach notification if information is presumed to have been "acquired." The weakest laws allow the company that failed to protect the consumer's information in the first place to decide whether to tell them, based on its estimate of the likelihood of identity theft or other harm. We call this a

---

[17] Robin Sidel and Daisuke Wakabayashi, "Apple Pay Stung by Low-Tech Fraudsters," 5 March 2015, Wall Street Journal, http://www.wsj.com/articles/apple-pay-stung-bylow-techfraudsters-1425603036 (last visited 15 March 2015).

"harm trigger." The worst harm triggers also define harm quite narrowly, when privacy advocates are well aware of the kinds of additional problems victimized consumers face.

Harms also include the cost and time spent cleaning these problems up, additional problems caused by an empty checking account or a missing tax refund and being denied or paying more for credit or insurance or rejected for jobs due to the digital carnage caused by the thief. Further, consumers face very real additional problems including the stigma of being branded a deadbeat and facing the emotional costs and worry that brings.

Only an acquisition standard will serve to force data collectors to protect the financial information of their trusted customers or accountholders well enough to avoid the costs, including to reputation, of a breach. Only if an entity's reputation is at risk will it do its best job to protect your reputation.

8) Any Bill That Purports to Protect Personally Identifiable Information Should Broadly Define Personal Information: Some federal data breach proposals define "Personally Identifiable Information" (PII) too narrowly. For example, under Florida's data security and breach notification law, the definition of personal information includes an email address and password combination.[18] Florida's law also protects a wide range of information about physical and mental health, medical history, and insurance, as do the state laws of California, Missouri, New Hampshire, North Dakota, Texas, and Virginia.[19] Many federal bills do not include protection for this sort of information in the event of a breach. Some state laws and proposed state laws may also include geolocation or marketing information in their definition of PII. Not all federal proposals consider these data points in their narrow definitions of protected PII. As a news release explained Illinois Attorney General Lisa Madigan's recent testimony to the U.S. Senate:

> "The Attorney General also testified that a federal data breach law must cover a broad range of sensitive data – not just social security numbers or stolen credit card numbers but also: online login credentials, medical information shared on the internet that is outside the scope of current privacy regulations, biometric data, and geolocation data. Companies must be required to report any data breach involving this type of personal information, Madigan said. Equally as important as Congress considers a federal data breach notification law, Madigan said, is the ability for state regulators to continue investigating data breaches at the state level. Federal legislation must not preempt the states' ability to respond and act when data breaches affect residents in their states. Any preemption by Congress must only provide a "floor" for reporting requirements and preserve a state's ability to use its consumer protection laws to investigate data security practices and enforce federal law.[20]"

---

[18] See http://www.leg.state.fl.us/statutes/index.cfm?App_mode=Display_Statute&Search_String=&URL=0500-0599/0501/Sections/0501.171.html

[19] See, for example, http://www.bakerlaw.com/files/Uploads/Documents/Data%20Breach%20documents/State_Data_Breach_Statute_Form.pdf

[20] Excerpt from news release "Madigan: Federal Data Breach Law Should Not Weaken States' Consumer Protections", 5 February 2015, available at http://www.illinoisattorneygeneral.gov/pressroom/2015_02/20150205.html (last visited 15 March 2015). General

9) Congress should further investigate marketing of overpriced credit monitoring and identity theft subscription products: In 2005 and then again in 2007 the FTC imposed fines on the credit bureau Experian for deceptive marketing of its various credit monitoring products, which are often sold as add-ons to credit cards and bank accounts. Banks receive massive commissions for selling them to their own customers. While it is likely that recent CFPB enforcement orders[21] against several large credit card companies for deceptive sale of the add-on products – resulting in refunds to date of over $1.5 billion to aggrieved consumers -- may cause banks to think twice about continuing these relationships with third-party firms, the committee should also consider its own examination of the sale of these credit card add-on products.

In addition to profits from credit monitoring, banks and other firms reap massive revenues from ID Theft insurance, sometimes sold in the same package and sometimes sold separately. Lifelock, a major 3rd party company in the identity protection space, was fined in 2010 for deceptive marketing, in an action brought by the FTC and 35 states.[22] Prices for these products from credit bureaus, Lifelock and others range up to $19.99/month. Companies that don't protect our information as the law requires add insult to injury by pitching us these over-priced monitoring and insurance products. The committee should call in the companies that provide ID theft insurance and force the industry to open its books and show what percentage of premiums are paid out to beneficiaries. It is probable that the loss ratio on these products is so low as to be meaningless, meaning profits are sky-high.

Consumers who want credit monitoring can monitor their credit themselves. No one should pay for it. You have the right under federal law to look at each of your 3 credit reports (Equifax, Experian and TransUnion) once a year for free at the federally-mandated central site annualcreditreport.com. Don't like websites? You can also access your federal free report rights by phone or email. You can stagger these requests – 1 every 4 months -- for a type of do-it-yourself no-cost monitoring. And, if you suspect you are a victim of identity theft, you can call each bureau directly for an additional free credit report. If you live in Colorado, Georgia, Massachusetts, Maryland, Maine, New Jersey, Puerto Rico or Vermont, you are eligible for yet another free report annually under state law by calling each of the Big 3 credit bureaus.

Madigan's testimony before the U.S. Senate Commerce Committee on that date is available at http://1.usa.gov/1tGFt5m (last visited 15 March 2015).

[21] We discuss some of the CFPB add-on cases here http://www.uspirg.org/blogs/eds-blog/usp/cfpb-gets-results-consumersand-taxpayers-too (last visited 15 March 2015).

[22] FTC, "LifeLock Will Pay $12 Million to Settle Charges by the FTC and 35 States That Identity Theft Prevention and Data Security Claims Were False," 9 March 2010, https://www.ftc.gov/news-events/press-releases/2010/03/lifelock-will-pay-12-million-settle-charges-ftc-35-states (last visited 15 March 2015).

Although federal authority against unfair monitoring marketing was improved in the 2009 Credit CARD Act,[23] the committee should also ask the regulators whether any additional changes are needed.

10) Congress Should Review Title V of the Gramm-Leach-Bliley Act and its Data Security Requirements: The 1999 Gramm-Leach-Bliley Act imposed modest data security responsibilities on regulated financial institutions, a broader category than simply banks. The requirements include breach notification, but only in certain risk-determined circumstances.[24] The committee should ask the regulators for information on their enforcement of these requirements and should determine whether additional legislation is needed, especially in light of the recent JP Morgan Chase breach. The committee should also recognize, as noted above, that mere compliance with weak GLBA guidance should not constitute constructive compliance with any additional security duties imposed on other players in the card network system as that could lead to a system where those other non-financial-institution players are treated unfairly.

11) Congress Must Not Weaken the Communication Act's Broad Privacy Protections: Leading consumer and privacy groups are also concerned that the powerful phone and cable companies seek to convince Congress to serve them, not the public interest, by using data breach legislation as an opportunity to move yet another Trojan Horse provision. They seek to weaken existing privacy protections for telephone metadata under Customer Proprietary Network Information (CPNI) regulations. They seek to rescind important provisions of the Communications Act that protect the personal information of telecommunications, cable, and satellite customers.[25]

V. A Threat to Consumers Is Posed by the Basic Business Model of the Digital Data Advertising Ecosystem

This testimony focuses primarily on the impact of a failure to secure consumer information. Congress should also investigate the broader problem of the over-collection of consumer information for marketing, tracking and predictive purposes. While the digital advertising ecosystem expands the number of vectors for misuse, the ubiquitous tracking of consumers poses threats as a business model itself.

---

[23] The Credit Card Accountability, Responsibility and Disclosure (CARD) Act of 2009, Public Law 111-24. See Section 205.

[24] See the Federal Financial Institutions Examination Council's "Final Guidance on Response Programs: Guidance on Response Programs for Unauthorized Access to Customer Information and Customer Notice,"2005, available at http://www.fdic.gov/news/news/financial/2005/fil2705.html

[25] Also see, re Communications Act, testimony of Laura Moy, New America Foundation, at a Hearing on a Discussion Draft of HR ___, Data Security and Breach Notification Act of 2015, Subcommittee on Commerce, Manufacturing, and Trade, U.S. House of Representatives, 18 March 2015, available at http://energycommerce.house.gov/hearing/discussion-draft-hr-data-security-and-breach-notification-act-2015 (last visited 16 March 2016).

In many ways, data breaches are the mere tip of the iceberg when it comes to privacy threats in the Big Data world.

In the Big Data world, companies are collecting vast troves of information about consumers. Every day, the collection and use of consumer information in a virtually unregulated marketplace is exploding. New technologies allow a web of interconnected businesses – many of which the consumer has never heard of – to assimilate and share consumer data in real-time for a variety of purposes that the consumer may be unaware of and may cause consumer harm. Increasingly, the information is being collected in the mobile marketplace and includes a new level of hyper-localized information.

The 1970 Fair Credit Reporting Act, for all its flaws our strongest privacy law, is largely based on the Code of Fair Information Practices.[26] Further, it limits the use of financial information for secondary purposes. The only marketing purposes allowed are credit and insurance marketing and then only after the law gives consumers the right to opt-out of those limited allowed uses.

Contrast the FCRA with the new Big Data uses of information which may not be fully regulated by the FCRA. The development of the Internet marketing ecosystem, populated by a variety of data brokers, advertising networks and other firms that collect, buy and sell consumer information without their knowledge and consent, is worthy of much greater Congressional inquiry.[27] The Federal Trade Commission has called for additional legislation to rein in the practices of largely unregulated data brokers. Here is a brief excerpt from the FTC's release accompanying its 2014 report:[28]

> Data brokers obtain and share vast amounts of consumer information, typically behind the scenes, without consumer knowledge. Data brokers sell this information for marketing campaigns and fraud prevention, among other purposes. Although consumers benefit from data broker practices which, for example, help enable consumers to find and enjoy the products and services they prefer, data broker practices also raise privacy concerns. [...] Among the report's findings:
> -- Data brokers collect consumer data from extensive online and offline sources, largely without consumers' knowledge, ranging from consumer purchase data, social media activity, warranty registrations, magazine subscriptions, religious and political affiliations, and other details of consumers' everyday lives.[...]

---

[26] Bob Gellman, "Fair Information Practices: A Basic History"," 11 February 2015, available at http://bobgellman.com/rg-docs/rg-FIPShistory.pdf (last visited 15 March 2015) Advocates consider the 1980 OECD version to be the best application of the FIPs.

[27] See the FTC's March 2012 report, "Protecting Consumer Privacy in an Era of Rapid Change: Recommendations For Businesses and Policymakers," available at http://www.ftc.gov/news-events/press-releases/2012/03/ftc-issues-final-commission-report-protecting-consumer-privacy. Also see Edmund Mierzwinski and Jeff Chester, "Selling Consumers, Not Lists: The New World of Digital Decision-Making and the Role of the Fair Credit Reporting Act," 46 Suffolk University Law Review Vol. 3, page 845 (2013), available at http://suffolklawreview.org/selling-consumers-not-lists/ (last visited 15 March 2015).

[28] Federal Trade Commission, "FTC Recommends Congress Require the Data Broker Industry to be More Transparent and Give Consumers Greater Control Over Their Personal Information," 27 May 2014, available at https://www.ftc.gov/news-events/press-releases/2014/05/ftc-recommends-congress-require-data-broker-industry-be-more (last visited 16 March 2015).

-- Data brokers combine and analyze data about consumers to make inferences about them, including potentially sensitive inferences such as those related to ethnicity, income, religion, political leanings, age, and health conditions. Potentially sensitive categories from the study are "Urban Scramble" and "Mobile Mixers," both of which include a high concentration of Latinos and African-Americans with low incomes. The category "Rural Everlasting" includes single men and women over age 66 with "low educational attainment and low net worths." Other potentially sensitive categories include health-related topics or conditions, such as pregnancy, diabetes, and high cholesterol.

Dramatic changes are transforming the U.S. financial marketplace. Far-reaching capabilities of "Big-Data" processing that gather, analyze, predict, and make instantaneous decisions about an individual; technological innovation spurring new and competitive financial products; the rapid adoption of the mobile phone as the principal online device; and advances in e-commerce and marketing that change the way we shop and buy, are creating a new landscape that holds both potential promise and risks for economically vulnerable Americans.[29]

VI. Conclusion: Consumers Need A Real Consumer Privacy Bill of Rights

Recently, the administration proposed a Consumer Privacy Bill of Rights. The original administration blueprint, in 2012, was encouraging.[30] However, this month we joined many other consumer and privacy groups,[31] and even leaders of the Federal Trade Commission,[32] an independent agency, in criticizing the approach taken in the draft, which appears to allow all existing marketplace practices, no matter how abusive or intrusive, to continue.

Congress has failed to address numerous digital threats to consumers, from data breaches to data brokers running amok to the very architecture of the digital ecosystem, where nearly every company -- known and unknown -- is tracking consumers, building a dossier on them and even auctioning them off to the highest bidder in real time (for advertising or financial offers).

Any data security, breach or privacy legislation should provide individuals with meaningful and enforceable control over the collection, use and sharing of their personal information.

---

[29] This paragraph is taken from a 2014 report, Edmund Mierzwinski and Jeff Chester, "Big Data Means Big Opportunities and Big Challenges", 27 March 2014, U.S. PIRG and the Center for Digital Democracy, available at http://www.uspirg.org/reports/usf/big-data-means-big-opportunities-and-big-challenges (last visited 16 March 2015).

[30] The White House, "We Can't Wait: Obama Administration Unveils Blueprint for a "Privacy Bill of Rights" to Protect Consumers Online," 12 February 2012, available at https://www.whitehouse.gov/the-press-office/2012/02/23/we-can-t-wait-obama-administration-unveils-blueprint-privacy-bill-rights (last visited 15 March 2015).

[31] Letter from Consumer and Privacy Groups to Congress Opposing Draft Administration Consumer Privacy Bill of Rights, 3 March 2015, available at http://www.consumerwatchdog.org/resources/ltrobamagroups030315.pdf (last visited 15 March 2015).

[32] FTC Commissioner Julie Brill is quoted by Rich Lord in the Pittsburgh Post-Gazette, "FTC Commissioner Brill, privacy advocate, 'disappointed' with White House proposal," 8 March 2015, available at http://www.post-gazette.com/news/nation/2015/03/08/FTC-Commissioner-Brill-privacy-advocate-disappointed-with-White-House-proposal/stories/201503080132 (last visited 15 March 2015). Chairwoman Edith Ramirez also made public criticisms.

Any bill should become a federal floor that upholds state privacy and data security laws, grants strong regulatory and enforcement authority to the Federal Trade Commission and state officials and allows states to continue to act as privacy leaders. Congress should give the Federal Trade Commission (FTC) adequate resources to protect privacy.

Any bill should adequately define what constitutes sensitive information, and provide consumers with meaningful choices about this data (ideally an opt-in to any secondary use). Any bill should protect large categories of personal information, including geolocation data, health records and marketing data collected on or off line. There should be no exceptions for business records, data "generally available to the public," and cyber threat indicators.

Proposed bills should not give companies leeway to determine the protections that consumers will receive. Most proposed bills' protections apply only if a company identifies a "context" or risk of harm. Protections should not be conditioned in such a way. Companies should face the threat of public exposure for failing to protect customer information.

As Congress considers amendments to address all the issues highlighted in this testimony, from data breaches to data security to data brokers and the Internet advertising ecosystem, it needs to consider any reforms in the context of the strongest possible application of the Code of Fair Information Practices discussed above.

Thank you for the opportunity to provide the Committee with our views. We are happy to provide additional information to Members or staff.

Committee on Oversight and Government Reform
Witness Disclosure Requirement – "Truth in Testimony"
Required by House Rule XI, Clause 2(g)(5)

Name: Edmund Mierzwinski, U.S. PIRG

1. Please list any federal grants or contracts (including subgrants or subcontracts) you have received since October 1, 2012. Include the source and amount of each grant or contract.

NONE

2. Please list any entity you are testifying on behalf of and briefly describe your relationship with these entities.

I am fulltime staff for U.S. Public Interest Research Group. I serve as Consumer Program Director. I have worked there for 25 years. U.S. PIRG is a non-profit, non-partisan organization.

3. Please list any federal grants or contracts (including subgrants or subcontracts) received since October 1, 2012, by the entity(ies) you listed above. Include the source and amount of each grant or contract.

NONE

I certify that the above information is true and correct.

Signature:
Date: 16 March 2015

U.S. PIRG
Federation of State PIRGs

January 2015

Biography of Edmund Mierzwinski, U.S. PIRG Consumer Program Director and Senior Fellow

Ed Mierzwinski has worked in the Washington, DC-based federal lobbying office of the Federation of State Public Interest Research Groups (U.S. PIRG) since 1989. He often lectures or testifies before Congress, state legislatures and agencies on a wide range of consumer issues, from credit card rates and privacy to product safety and airline passenger rights. He has published reports on numerous consumer issues, including Big Data's impact on financial opportunity, the CFPB Public Consumer Complaint Database, internet privacy, identity theft and credit reporting mistakes. He is co-author of a Model State Data Breach, Security Freeze and Identity Theft Law available on SSRN. He has had recent articles in the *American Prospect,* the *Journal of Consumer Affairs* and the *Suffolk University Law Review.*

He is a 2003 recipient of Privacy International's "Brandeis Award" for privacy protection efforts and a 2006 recipient of the Consumer Federation of America's "Esther Peterson Consumer Service Award." For the last 5 years, "The Hill" newspaper has selected him as a "Top Lobbyist" awardee and, in 2011, *Bloomberg Businessweek* selected him as one of "15 Power Brokers: Regulators, lawmakers and lobbyists shaping the torrent of regulations."

In August 2012, he was re-elected to a second 3-year term on the board of directors of Consumer Reports (formerly Consumers Union), the world's largest consumer product testing and advocacy organization. He chairs the Americans for Financial Reform (AFR) Consumer Financial Protection Bureau Task Force. He is a founding and current member of the Steering Committee of the Transatlantic Consumer Dialogue (tacd.org). He is on the board of directors of Flyersrights.org. He is a former member of the Federal Reserve Board's Consumer Advisory Council. He is a graduate of the University of Connecticut (BA, MS) and previously was Executive Director of the Connecticut PIRG.

Ed Mierzwinski, edm@pirg.org or direct line 202-461-3821
Ed's blog, http://www.uspirg.org/consumer-blog Twitter @edmpirg

---

U.S. Public Interest Research Group, 218 D St SE, Washington, DC 20003
Phone 202-546-9707 Fax 202-546-2461

Mr. HURD. Thank you, Mr. Mierzwinski.

I now recognize Mr. Walker from North Carolina for 5 minutes of questioning.

Mr. WALKER. Thank you, Mr. Chairman.

This is a lot of information to process. It is very studious work on your parts. I appreciate that.

I have two or three things I want to address. Mr. Nutkis, let me start with you.

I have a lot of family in the health care industry. More and more that is becoming technological. Concerns and challenges facing this industry when addressing cyber threats is that something that has come across the table as far as discussion?

I want to know what you are hearing on this and how you would address it? Is it a problem that you are hearing or facing in the medical community?

Mr. NUTKIS. Cyber threats specific to medical devices?

Mr. WALKER. Correct, yes.

Mr. NUTKIS. Absolutely. That has been an ongoing issue. We were the first to start tracking vulnerabilities associated with medical devices. We see them on two sides, the implantable and the non-implantable as well as the control systems that are associated or controlling the devices as well. It is an ongoing problem.

At this point, we do not track an exorbitant number of threats associated with them but there is no question we track vulnerabilities.

Mr. WALKER. At some point, is this considered a life and death matter? Could someone hack a system where they increase the defibrillator or are we at that point to be concerned about that?

Mr. NUTKIS. There have been demonstrations where, in fact, that has occurred. The circumstances are very specific. The answer is absolutely.

The likelihood based on all the circumstances that would have to occur, there is no question this is a concern, disruption of life. One of the things we do is look at risk assessments and the analysis. We escalate from the PII to the PHI to sensitive health information to other types of information, the disruption of the facility itself to disruption of care.

It goes beyond the device. You have electronic health records systems used for ordering. What if people start removing your drug allergies from your systems and you have contraindication.

I think these are all being worked on. We actually created a new working group specifically to look at better disclosure and how to move along this process.

Mr. WALKER. Mr. Bejtlich, earlier I believe you categorized different cyber attacks by the Chinese and Russians were for financial purposes. Can you go through that process again? I want to make sure I get that information because you said some of it was financial and some was more malicious intent. You make sure I have all that information correct?

Mr. BEJTLICH. At the top, the nation-State end, you see the Russians, the Chinese, increasingly now the North Koreans and the Iranians.

The problems you discussed with health care, that could come from any sector. It could be a criminal element, an activist element and so forth.

Briefly, we do have part of an answer. That is in the security community specifically with researchers. Part of the problem they are encountering is some of the research they do could be construed as hacking and put them at risk of being prosecuted simply for trying to identify these vulnerabilities.

We need to create a safe space for that sort of work.

Mr. WALKER. In your opinion, if you are looking at lone wolf, guy on the mountain based criminal behavior versus some of the international threats, give me a concern overall in your community as far as what we are looking at? Where is the weightedness as far as immediate concern we are.

Mr. BEJTLICH. From the chronic theft of intellectual property, business methods and that sort of thing, I care about the Chinese the most. If I care about geo-political problems that could leak from the physical area, I worry about the Russians and what is going on in Ukraine and their using cyber capability to deter or back up something they are doing physically.

Mr. WALKER. Do you have any numbers as far as how many attacks we might be trying fiend off on a daily basis?

Mr. BEJTLICH. The best number I gave, sir, was the 3,000. Those are not trivial hacks caused by someone in a basement. Those are serious intruders that are tracked on a campaign basis by the FBI.

Mr. WALKER. Before my time expires, you mentioned three things earlier as far as working to prevent some of this, better credit cards. Can you address some of that? What do you mean by that?

Mr. FRENCH. Better payment card security. The card security choices have been made by the card industry and the banks. Part of it is hardening the card, putting a chip on the card and that is going on currently.

As Mr. Mierzwinski noted, the banks are choosing to use chip and signature, not chip and pin. The only really effective method of authenticating and individual is a pin.

A system also needs end to end encryption as well as tokenization. Ultimately you want to take the number out of the system so that the number cannot be captured and replicated.

Mr. WALKER. Thank you, Mr. Chairman. I yield back.

Mr. HURD. Thank you, Mr. Walker.

I now recognize the Ranking Member, Ms. Kelly, from Illinois.

Ms. KELLY. Thank you, Mr. Chairman.

In a survey of health care providers published last year, the Ponemon Institute found ''90 percent of health care organizations in the study have had at least one data breach in the past 2 years.''

A New York Times article that was published stated, ''Health organizations like Anthem are likely to be vulnerable targets because they have been slower to adopt measures like keeping personal information in separate data bases that can be closed off in an attack. They are generally less secure than financial services companies with the same type of customer data.''

Mr. Nutkis, as the CEO of an organization that works with many leading health care organizations to improve their data security, what are the most pressing challenges the industry faces when it comes to securing the personal data of its patients from cyber thieves?

Mr. NUTKIS. That is a question we deal with all the time. We have a maturity problem. We have a resource problem. I think we have seen the two of them come together.

I think we have done a good job in moving the yardsticks with regard to industry's maturity. We have seen large organizations implement stronger security controls. I think it is important to note we do this on a risk basis, meaning that we assume health care data is never going to be as well protected as launch codes to a nuclear silo or payloads.

I think there is an expectation that there is always an amount of risk. Certainly we can do a much better job. We have tried to do this with education and bringing in tools. One of the things we are really transitioning from being a compliance-based industry, not a risk-based industry.

Our major focus, although we have known for many years that cyber was coming, we had regulations to comply with in regard to HIPPA privacy and people were spending more resources on those things because the data supported a privacy breach versus a security breach.

Where do you spend your resources? You look at the top ten list. You focus on privacy. I think we have seen this transition very quickly to security. I think now we are seeing organizations take it seriously.

It would certainly help, and we have looked for, a degree of safe harbor. You do the right things, you implement the right controls, you get management support to get the funding, and when you do that, if something happens, which will happen by the way in some cases, you did everything you could.

Right now, by the way, organizations look at Anthem, look at other organizations that did extremely well. They were able to detect it themselves, they communicated quickly and have done a number of things. They go, well if Anthem cannot protect themselves, we do not have a chance.

I think we are trying to let them know that is not the case. There is a lot that you can do. As a matter of fact, as those other organizations start to build stronger security measures, you are going to be a bigger target because you are all that is left.

Ms. KELLY. Would you cite the reasons you just shared with us for the health care industry being technologically behind other industries because of where the focus has been and the resources have gone?

Mr. NUTKIS. I think there are two reasons. One certainly is the resources, no question about it. The other, I think to some degree, is we have a lot of organizations. We have at least 400,000 directly in the industry and some that are sole practitioners, two doc practices, so I think when you get below the first 50,000 in the industry, you are really talking about very resource challenged.

I think a lot of what we have tried to do is figure out how to move the maturity. Unfortunately, they are all interconnected. The small doc's practice still gets access to the same records that the health plan or hospital has. You end up with a big weak link problem. We have really tried to move that. We see it as a resource problem and also a priority problem.

Ms. KELLY. What would be your key recommendations for improving the apparent security vulnerabilities?

Mr. NUTKIS. Our recommendations are providing a degree of safe harbor, recognizing organizations that implement strong security controls, and get assessed against those controls to demonstrate, in fact, that they are doing everything they can.

The State of Texas is a good example. Texas has something called Secure Texas which if you comply with and get certified, you get a degree of liability protection if something happens. Organizations seem to be very receptive and see that as the right way to go get the funding they need.

We look at information sharing as a great approach. I think it important to note that to some degree—look at the Premera breach yesterday or even the Anthem breach—the information that is being shared is quite old. Those breaches occurred in a period of time previously.

Also, we are still trying to work with the vendor community. It is a $68 billion market of information security products. We would like to see them step up more as well. The small organizations do not have a chance in being able to affect the save way and the budgets are not the same. They are going to have to rely more on existing product.

Ms. KELLY. How can Congress help you? How can we be of assistance?

Mr. NUTKIS. We would be very supportive of things like safe harboring, giving organizations the ability to do the right things, understand what they are, and implement them.

We certainly are in favor of information sharing but again, if you do not have mature organizations, you end up with bad data being shared which really does not help anyone. We are hoping we get the controls in place. People can adopt those controls which force more mature organizations, more mature organizations can more effectively share.

I think we have seen a lot of large organizations in industry being willing to share. We have seen the new bill supporting that. We think that is moving along. We see liability protection with regard to safe harbors being the way to get the whole process started.

Once everyone starts getting more mature, there is better sharing, less risk and the whole model comes together.

Ms. KELLY. Thank you so much.

Thank you, Mr. Chair.

Mr. HURD. I recognize my colleague, Ms. Duckworth, from Illinois.

Ms. DUCKWORTH. Thank you, Mr. Chairman.

I would like to turn the discussion toward the concept of data minimization and data reduction as a security measure.

Mr. Bejtlich, could you speak a bit to this principle? Do you think that as a practice, if businesses adopted data minimization, would this type of security measure be more effective in mitigating the damage from a breach?

Mr. BEJTLICH. When you think in terms of risk, you have threat, vulnerability and the impact. To date, most of the focus has been on vulnerability. The problem is vulnerability is everywhere.

If we can take steps that make the data less valuable than if there is a breach, when there is a breach, there will not be that much of an impact. Furthermore, we should look at ways for recovery. In other words, we are looking at what can we do to stop a breach from happening but we need to look at once the breach has happened, what happens next. Who is responsible for cleanup the mess of an identity theft? How much does it cost?

There is a misalignment of a lot of these issues so it falls on the consumer and the citizen. Many times they are in the worse position to try to affect change.

Ms. DUCKWORTH. Can you speak a bit to the role of encryption in protecting highly sensitive data, especially on business and agency networks? This committee's job is to provide oversight of business and government agencies. Can you speak a bit to encryption?

I also sit on Armed Services and am looking at some of their encryption challenges, especially with significant numbers of sub-contractors, sub-subcontractors and the like.

Mr. BEJTLICH. Encryption has a value in certain areas. If I am going to talk to a colleague at the end of the table and want to make sure no one in between can hear it, I want to encrypt that data.

If I am carrying around data on an external hard drive or a thumb drive and I lose it in a taxi, I want to make sure that is encrypted.

Encryption stops the intruder from getting access to it. In certain areas encryption can be useful but we have to remember that in order for data to be useful, it has to be read at some point. Encryption will not necessarily be valuable at the point where that data is being used.

Ms. DUCKWORTH. Following this train of thought, I would like to look at data segmentation. We have talked about data minimization and encryption. Let us talk about data segmentation.

Mr. Johnson, can you talk about this as a practice in your industry, if it is considered a best practice, and what would be happening if more businesses chose to do data segmentation?

Mr. JOHNSON. I think it is really systems segmentation when you look at it. I think we have seen a number of breaches both within our industry and in the merchant industry and others where segmentation has not occurred and you have been able to get into a separate system because there was an ability to enter into a different system.

An example might be an air conditioning vendor in the case of Target and in the case of a financial institution, I know of a work file going into human resources that ended up compromising an ATM system.

It is very, very important to learn those lessons that you have segmentation between those systems and only authorize access to data and substantial rights protections associated with who has the right to that data, to view that data and change that data.

I think we spend a lot of time in our industry thinking through that and our regulatory agencies do as well. One of the major findings that the regulatory agencies came up with based upon their 500 audits they did last year of community banks was there was absolutely undue complication within financial systems.

There were things plugged into other things that did not need to be plugged in to other things. There was connectivity issues associated with systems.

One of the charges we have based on that is to look and make sure our systems are not unduly complicated so that we do not unduly add data and potentially be compromised because of that.

Ms. DUCKWORTH. Mr. Bejtlich, could you speak a bit to the cooperation between the Chinese government and their business sector in conducting cyber espionage? Specifically, I am thinking of the case where there were Chinese companies that infiltrated Lockheed Martin, stole a lot of data and shared that data with the Chinese government which then resulted in their upgrading their fifth generation fighter jets.

Can you talk a bit about that partnership that seems to be occurring?

Mr. BEJTLICH. There is collaboration among different elements of the Chinese hacking scene. You have top end military units, militia units, quasi-military and then you have the patriotic hackers.

There is certainly a career progress that people go through. As far as the tasking goes, the military units are tasked to go after private sector companies in the west to steal intellectual property, business methods and that sort of data.

Ms. DUCKWORTH. Thank you.

Mr. HURD. Thank you.

Votes have been called on the floor but I believe we can make it through questioning so the witnesses will not have to wait around during the vote series.

With that, I would recognize the Ranking Member of the Oversight and Government Reform Committee, Mr. Cummings, from Maryland.

Mr. CUMMINGS. Mr. Chairman, I will be brief because I know you want to get to your questions.

First of all, I want to welcome you to your chairmanship and to the committee. I want to thank our Ranking Member. Congratulations to both of you.

The issue of cyber security has been one which I have been trying to raise before this committee for years. I give credit to you and Chairman Chaffetz for addressing it now because it is so very, very important.

I have a lot of questions but I want to let the Chairman ask his questions.

I sit on the Naval Academy Board of Trustees and Board of Visitors. We understand that cyber security is so very important. We have done a lot to make sure that all of our midshipmen are exposed to cyber security education.

Do you think that we are preparing our Nation and our young people and the troops to be able to effectively deal with this very, very serious threat to our way of life, to our existence?

Right now, we are dealing with the Secret Service. You see situations where people say we are prepared but when it comes time for the rubber to meet the road, you discover there is no road.

I am wondering how you all feel about our colleges, universities and other institutions? Are we where we need to be to effectively deal with this serious problem?

Mr. BEJTLICH. Sir, I can address that. I am from the Air Force Academy class of 1994. I maintain contact with my colleagues there. Also, I have been to beautiful Annapolis.

At the service academies you do see very strong focus on cyber security. There are contests between the different academies.

Outside of that, at the regular universities and such, as my generation moves into teaching, you are seeing more focus on what we have done in corporate America in dealing with intruders, less focus on more abstract topics like cryptography, which has a role, but it is not the same thing as the rubber meeting the road that you mentioned. I think that situation is getting better.

I would like to also mention CyberPatriot. This is a program for middle school and high school students nationwide. In my kids' school just won the national championship for the middle schools.

There is a focus now that is both generational and also at different levels of schools, not just at the colleges but we are seeing that migrate down to the middle schools. I would not be surprised if there a one through five program coming up next.

Mr. CUMMINGS. Thank you, Mr. Chairman.

Mr. HURD. Mr. Cummings, I appreciate your being here today and your leadership on this committee.

I now recognize myself for 5 minutes for questioning.

The first question goes to Mr. French, Mr. Nutkis and Mr. Johnson. Can you talk to me about the top two digital threats to your industry and the folks you represent, the kind of threat actor whether it is a country or a specific individual or a person looking for a particular type of information?

Mr. FRENCH. From the pattern of breaches that we have seen in recent years, it is organized gangs of criminals using very sophisticated attacks generally originating in Eastern Europe. I think that is the pattern we have seen almost in every instance.

Unfortunately, they have a very sophisticated method of doing this and wipe their tracks when they go in. It is very difficult. They know what we are looking for and it is very difficult for us to track them inside our systems and wipe them out.

Mr. HURD. Mr. Nutkis?

Mr. NUTKIS. I think we see it in two ways, assuming by the way that we protected it to begin with, in the first, but I think we found with the Chinese they are there so long and so stealthy that the damage is substantial. When they get in, you are seeing much larger breaches or we are not seeing them at all because they are getting in and out.

We are also seeing from Russia more financial. There is either some sort of extortion or financial. They are less methodical, so they leave a lot more trails.

Those two for us are the ones we see the most.

Mr. JOHNSON. Unfortunately, sir, we see them all. Of course during the service attacks, those were political, so those were from a nation State. From the Chinese, we see the intellectual property thefts. From the criminals, regardless whether or not they are attacking for economic gain, any set of breached data it is going to be a bank customer we end up reimbursing at the end of the line for potential financial loss.

We become increasingly concerned about threats that have the potential of manipulating or destroying data. When does data disruption become data destruction is what we spend a lot of time thinking about in terms of ensuring we do not have data with the capacity to be manipulated.

You hear about advanced persistent threats a lot. I think there are more irritating persistent threats, IPTs, because they do not necessarily have a level of advancement, they just happen to be there for very extended periods of time over time. We see a great deal of patience among all these perpetrators.

Mr. HURD. Mr. Bejtlich, in our opinion, I know your firm deals with all of the above threats. Is the Federal Government prepared to help private industry and the private sector in fighting these issues?

Mr. BEJTLICH. We have seen in recent high profile breaches, the FBI ready to assist. I do not know their ability to scale, however. I am not sure if we were to send the Bureau to every one of the breaches that my company is working, whether they would become quickly overwhelmed.

That is one of the areas where this is different than a physical situation where you can call your local police and they are usually equipped to help you. We do not yet have a scalable government response to the problem.

Mr. HURD. Mr. French, Mr. Nutkis and Mr. Johnson, very quickly, in what ways can the government better provide information to you or what type of information should the government be providing to you to help protect your industry and the folks you represent?

Mr. FRENCH. The government could do two things, in our opinion. First, better cyber sharing legislation would help to facilitate more real time exchange of information so that parties within the economy would be sharing with each other.

The government has, through many of their systems, whether it is US-CERT or the Secret Service or FBI, done a very good job of working with, for example, Mr. Johnson's FS-ISAC. The FS-ISAC is a very sophisticated means of flowing that information out. They use a traffic light protocol that shares that information with parties and partners in the industry including retailers.

The information flow is there but we could use some cyber security legislation.

Mr. HURD. Mr. Nutkis, briefly.

Mr. NUTKIS. I think for us it is the format of the information. We would like more information that is more valuable, accurate information and we would like it in a format that we can get to the consumer quickly.

There is a lot of work involved and a lot of it is information. The analogy I use is Amazon online, Hulu Plus and Netflix. We are getting the same information over and over again. We really just want the stuff we want, so specify what is really important.

If you end up with too much information, people get distracted, so we need good information and we need it in a format that we can distribute quickly.

Mr. HURD. Mr. Johnson, you have 30 seconds.

Mr. JOHNSON. First of all, let the record show that I completely agree with Mr. French on this issue regarding information sharing.

Second, I think liability protection is the other piece of that because we need clarity in terms of what that liability protection for voluntary sharing information is, recognizing proper privacy protections need to be in place, and data needs to be minimized.

I think that would greatly enhance the ability of us to have more adequate information sharing across sectors particularly.

Mr. HURD. I would like to recognize Ms. Kelly for 2 minutes.

Ms. KELLY. Mr. Mierzwinski, since not everyone is familiar with the crime of medical identity theft, can you explain to us what it is, how it occurs, and then what type of personal information do cyber thieves target when they commit medical identity theft?

Mr. MIERZWINSKI. The medical identity theft is a relatively newly identified problem. The World Privacy Forum has issued several reports on it. Essentially, instead of opening bank accounts in your name, somebody obtains medical services in your name. They may not be able to afford health insurance but they use your health insurance to get the services that they cannot afford.

It is a very significant problem. Again, for the first time, we understand that the Anthem breach did not include medical service information but the Premera breach may have. The Anthem breach, however, provided enough information to commit all the other kinds of identity theft and possibly to apply for health insurance in your name.

Ms. KELLY. Thank you so much.

Thank you, Mr. Chairman.

Mr. HURD. Gentlemen, I wish we had two or three more hours to continue this conversation. This is an important topic and something I am looking forward to working with Ranking Member Kelly on.

I really appreciate you all taking the time to appear before us today. The materials you provided in advance were incredibly helpful as well. I am looking forward to following up with each of you individually on that as we chart a course on making sure the Federal Government is doing absolutely everything we can to protect our consumers and our industries from those trying to do us ill.

If there is no further business, without objection, the subcommittee stands adjourned.

[Whereupon, at 2:03 p.m., the subcommittee was adjourned.]